I have never read another book that deals with the full range of brain traps. When you hear the term "soul ties," you think of ungodly emotional ties to other people. But it's far more diabolical. Soul ties can be ungodly addictions or lust of all kinds, such as food, television, drugs, adultery, pornography, or even hobbies such as sports. All and more can be idolatry and open you up to spirits of darkness. Finally, a book that identifies the problem and is the "go to" book for complete freedom. Every Christian should have this resource in their library.

SID ROTH
Host, *It's Supernatural*

DESTINY IMAGE BOOKS BY DENNIS AND JENNIFER CLARK

Flowing in the River of God's Will

A Practical Guide to Self-Deliverance

Releasing the Divine Healer Within

The Supernatural Power of Peace

Deep Relief Now: Free, Healed, and Whole

Live Free

Breaking Soul Ties

Visit Drs. Dennis and Jennifer Clark online at www.forgive123.com.

Visit the online school directed by Jason Clark at http://training.teamembassy.com.

Jason's full testimony is available as *Grace Transforms* in CD and DVD format at www.forgive123.com.

breaking
SOUL TIES

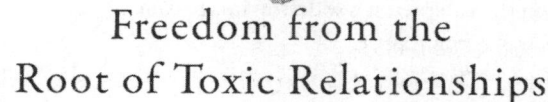

Freedom from the
Root of Toxic Relationships

DRS. DENNIS & JENNIFER CLARK
with Jason Clark

© Copyright 2019 – Dennis and Jennifer Clark

All rights reserved. This book is protected by the copyright laws of the United States of America. This book may not be copied or reprinted for commercial gain or profit. The use of short quotations or occasional page copying for personal or group study is permitted and encouraged. Permission will be granted upon request. Unless otherwise identified, Scripture quotations are from the New King James Version. Copyright © 1982 by Thomas Nelson. Used by permission. All rights reserved. Scripture quotations marked AMPC are from the Amplified® Bible Classic Edition, Copyright © 1954, 1958, 1962, 1964, 1965, 1987 by The Lockman Foundation, La Habra, CA 90631. All rights reserved. Used by permission. Scripture quotations marked KJV are from the King James Version. Scripture quotations marked MSG are from The Message. Copyright © 1993, 1994, 1995, 1996, 2000, 2001, 2002. Used by permission of NavPress Publishing Group. Scripture quotations marked NLT are from the Holy Bible, New Living Translation, copyright © 1996, 2004, 2015 by Tyndale House Foundation. Used by permission of Tyndale House Publishers Inc., Carol Stream, Illinois 60188. All rights reserved. Scripture quotations marked NASB are from the NEW AMERICAN STANDARD BIBLE®, Copyright © 1960, 1962, 1963, 1968, 1971, 1972, 1973, 1975, 1977, 1995 by The Lockman Foundation. Used by permission. Emphasis within Scripture is the authors' own.

DESTINY IMAGE® PUBLISHERS, INC.

P.O. Box 310, Shippensburg, PA 17257-0310
"Promoting Inspired Lives."

This book and all other Destiny Image and Destiny Image Fiction books are available at Christian bookstores and distributors worldwide.

Cover design by Eileen Rockwell
Interior design by Terry Clifton

For more information on foreign distributors, call 717-532-3040.
Or reach us on the Internet: www.destinyimage.com

ISBN 13 TP: 978-0-7684-4833-7
ISBN 13 EBook: 978-0-7684-4834-4
ISBN LP: 978-0-7684-4835-1
ISBN HC: 978-0-7684-4836-8

For Worldwide Distribution, Printed in the U.S.A.
1 2 3 4 5 6 / 22 21 20 19

Contents

SECTION ONE	UNDERSTANDING SOUL TIES	1
Chapter One	Caught in a Trap	3
Chapter Two	Spirit, Soul, and Body	9
Chapter Three	Created for Relationship	17
Chapter Four	What Is a Soul Tie?	31
Chapter Five	The Tangled Web of Codependency	49
SECTION TWO	FINDING FREEDOM	61
Chapter Six	Spiritual Anatomy	63
Chapter Seven	Dealing with Emotions	75
Chapter Eight	Dislodging Troublesome Thoughts	87
Chapter Nine	Filling Emotional Need	95
SECTION THREE	DEALING WITH HABITS	109
Chapter Ten	Life, Purpose, and Traps	111
Chapter Eleven	Breaking Bad Habits	119
Chapter Twelve	The Habit of Prayer	133
SECTION FOUR	HEALING FOR SEXUAL ISSUES	145
Chapter Thirteen	God's Word, Will, and Way	147
Chapter Fourteen	The Science of Love	167
Chapter Fifteen	Lust and Brain Traps	187
Chapter Sixteen	The Pornography Epidemic	195
SECTION FIVE	WALKING IT OUT	207
Chapter Seventeen	Church as Family	209
Chapter Eighteen	Remapping the Brain	215
Chapter Nineteen	Restoration	225

Section One

UNDERSTANDING SOUL TIES

Chapter 1

CAUGHT IN A TRAP
by Jason

Our soul has escaped as a bird from the snare of the fowlers; the snare is broken, and we have escaped.
—Psalm 124:7

How had it ever come to this? Everything had started out so well! She was sweet, cute, and exactly my type. And, just what I thought I'd ever wanted—my Proverbs 31 woman. I had fallen head-over-heels in love with Lana and, at first, really believed she could be "the one." Overcome with joy, I called my father (Dennis) to tell him all about her. Within a few months, however, I began voicing my fears and confusion to him as I got sucked into a swirling whirlpool of lies, torment, and madness. My dream girl became my captor and life became a nightmarish reality.

MY DREAM GIRL BECAME MY CAPTOR!

The truth started to be exposed when I caught her in all sorts of lies and deceptions, beginning with the fact that she was cheating on me with a former boyfriend. Soon things took a darker turn to physical abuse and emotional gaslighting, which is psychological manipulation designed to sow seeds of self-doubt making the targeted individual question their own memory, perception, and sanity.

Usually the perpetrator is deliberate, cunning, and sociopathic; however, in this case, it was Lana's own craziness, manipulation, and control that caused me to question my own sanity. I then threatened to leave her, at which point she turned me in to the cops and made false charges against me. Now we were locked into the legal system and I couldn't go anywhere else for at least a year while the wheels of local justice began to slowly grind.

Lana didn't want to lose me. After all, she had already moved into my apartment, quit her job, and convinced me to pay for all sorts of medications for mental and physical ailments, many of which were imaginary. Unfortunately, my rescuer identity and codependency took over. Now the lock on the trap snapped into place: Lana needed me. To cut her loose at this point would have seemed like kicking a wounded dog to the curb and walking away.

When I sought help from a psychiatrist, he did what doctors usually do—he wrote prescriptions to help alleviate my anxiety, depression, and other symptoms. I found myself taking all sorts of powerful medications to which I quickly became addicted but which only increased my torment. And Lana liked me doped up. It made it easier for her to control me and keep me from leaving her.

Still having enough presence of mind to document the physical abuse, I sent some photos of the stab wounds in my face from her keys and the bloody fingernail scratches across my cheeks and neck to Dad and Jennifer. All it took to set Lana off was my failure to do exactly what she wanted or to do something the wrong way, even if I didn't know what her "right way" was. The situation I described was bad, and they were very concerned about my welfare. Dad and Jen told me to leave her and move in with them because they had a place where I could stay until I could get my life sorted out. But, unable to act even on my fear, I wound myself even more tightly into what had become a web of my own making.

I WAS IN A WEB OF MY OWN MAKING.

The can of tomatoes broken over my head didn't do it. The bare foot Lana used to kick a hole through the bathroom door when I locked myself in didn't do it. The road incident was the last straw. Lana insisted that we go to the grocery store in the wee hours of the morning, even though I hadn't had any sleep that night and needed to leave for work at five-thirty. While she was driving to the store, she got angry and smacked me hard across the bridge of my nose with the back of her hand. I'd had enough.

Without warning, I abruptly unbuckled my seat belt, threw it off me, and yanked open the door to throw myself out of the moving car. My thinking was that I'd die or be hurt badly enough to be admitted to the hospital, but either possibility was better than being with Lana. Somehow, in a flash, she reached across me, grabbed the seat belt as the buckle hit the car window, and jerked me back with the belt as we swerved all over the road. This incident finally prompted me to take action. The realization that I had come close to death shook me. It was like ice water thrown in my face, shocking me awake. Something had to change, and it had to change fast.

Something had to change, and it had to change fast.

How could I leave the apartment and make my escape? The next morning, I let my father know I was coming and asked for his counsel. Dad contacted a police friend who said, "Tell him to call the police and ask for a police escort so he can get to his car. That way she can't call the police first and make false charges like she's done in the past."

Following Dad's advice, the police came at my request and escorted me out with nothing but my cell phone, what I had on, and my computer, which had tax information and other personal data I didn't want to get into the wrong hands. After driving a couple of days, I pulled up to my dad's front door.

It's great that I was able to physically escape from the horrible trap I was in, but the next thing I had to learn was how to stay free because, as I soon discovered, toxic soul ties once formed have a demonic, magnetic pull that tries to reattach. This whole pattern needed to be broken too because I had gone from one toxic relationship to another my entire adult life. It took this last one, however, to get me to rock-bottom.

As I turned to God in prayer, He began to work inside me. I needed internal as well as external liberation and the Lord met me at my point of need. In this book you will discover the secrets I learned on my journey to complete freedom and a brand-new life![1]

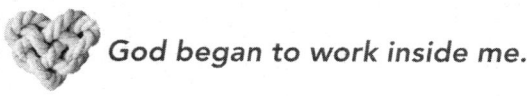 *God began to work inside me.*

God made my life complete when I placed all the pieces before him. When I cleaned up my act, he gave me a fresh start. ...God rewrote the text of my life when I opened the book of my heart to his eyes (2 Samuel 22:21-25 MSG).

ENDNOTE

1. Jason's full testimony is available as *Grace Transforms* in CD and DVD format on www.forgive123.com.

Chapter 2

Spirit, Soul, and Body

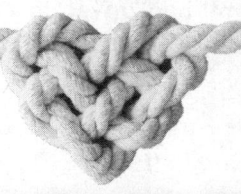

JASON'S STORY

After two days of driving, I arrived at my dad's house in a shell-shocked condition. I was emotionally wrecked. In my escape from Kansas City, I'd even failed to pack the powerful meds prescribed for a host of maladies (including PTSD, depression, and anxiety) and to which I was addicted. As a matter of fact, in the natural, it was extremely dangerous to quit cold-turkey. There must have been a special grace on me because I suffered no withdrawal symptoms at all.

The phone calls began immediately. Lana started calling my phone as well as Dad's landline and cell, maybe hundreds of times. It was crazy and frightening with all the tears and threats, but I felt inconceivably badly about leaving. She had once had a job and her own place, but, before long, I had started supporting her completely. I felt responsible for her.

Dad kept telling me she had already proved that she could take care of herself and that it was not my job to be her savior. He told me to cut all ties with her, concentrate on myself, and get my life turned around. To do that, it was necessary to change my phone number and email and all other avenues

> of possible communication. We also filed a police report and took other protective steps in case she followed me to South Carolina.
>
> The next thing I had to do was present all the junk hidden in my own heart to the Lord—the soulish issues that had driven me to such a desperate state. My backslidden condition with all its guilt and shame had driven me far from the presence of God. But, in response to my small steps back to Him, God came running to me!
>
> *Create in me a clean heart, O God; and renew a right spirit within me* (Psalm 51:10 KJV).

Although Jason was a preacher's kid who had grown up in church and graduated from Bible college, he needed to revisit the subject of spirit-soul-body, especially as it pertained to his wounded condition. Jason understood a great deal about prayer and communing with God, but far less about how the Lord deals with our soul to set us free from soul ties and toxic emotions. We experience wholeness only when Jesus is our Lord and rules all three areas.

Some theologians disagree about what the soul is, what the spirit of man is, and whether or not it is correct to make a distinction between the two. We do know that God created us to be a thinking, willing, feeling being; and all three of these faculties should be surrendered to the Holy Spirit. Adam, like us, was formed as a spirit, living in a material body, possessing a mind, will, and emotions—the soul.

WE ARE THINKING, WILLING, FEELING BEINGS.

The word "spirit" is used more than 900 times throughout the Scriptures, referring to God, angels, and demons. We have a human spirit. God is a Spirit. Since He created humans in His image, we are spirit beings as well. Adam and Eve had spirits that communed with God, their spirits touching the Spirit of God: *"He who is joined to the Lord is one spirit with Him"* (1 Corinthians 6:17).

Human beings are different from the rest of God's creation because they alone are made in the image of God. God said, *"Let Us make man in Our image, according to Our likeness"* (Genesis 1:26). *"God created man in His own image; in the image of God He created him; male and female He created them"* (Genesis 1:27).

Man is made up of physical material, the body, that can be seen and touched. But we are also made up of immaterial aspects, which are intangible—this includes the soul, spirit, intellect, will, emotions, conscience, and so forth. These immaterial characteristics exist beyond the physical lifespan of the human body and are therefore eternal.

These immaterial aspects—the spirit, soul, heart, conscience, mind, and emotions—make up the whole personality. The Bible makes it clear that the soul and spirit are the primary immaterial aspects of humanity, while the body is the physical container that holds them on this earth.[1]

SPIRIT, SOUL, AND BODY

Because we are spiritual beings who live on planet earth, we must be able to interact with the world around us. We are spirits with a soul who live in a body. With his physical body, Adam could feel the breeze blow and touch the plants placed in the Garden. Adam also had the ability to think and make choices—God let him choose the names of all of the animals that were created (see Genesis 2:18-20). And Adam also had emotions—he loved God and he felt God's love toward him.

God is a triune being, Father, Son, and Holy Spirit as three in one, and we are also tripartite beings—spirit, soul, and body. Apostle Paul writes clearly about these three parts of man:

> *Now may the God of peace Himself sanctify you completely; and may your whole spirit, soul, and body be preserved blameless at the coming of our Lord Jesus Christ* (1 Thessalonians 5:23).

 **We are tripartite beings—spirit, soul, and body.**

Watchman Nee calls man's spirit the inner man, the soul is the outer man, and the body the outermost man.² For our spirit to make contact with the world around us, our spirit needs to flow through our soul. This is what we commonly call the Lordship of Christ. In a sense, the soul can either imprison our spirit within us or release our spirit outwardly.

When Jesus controls our thoughts, choices, and feelings, He is ruling. Our spirit is free. However, when *we* control our thoughts, choices, and feelings, we are ruling. Our spirit is encased. "God intended for man's spirit to be His home or dwelling place. So the Holy Spirit making a union with the human spirit was to govern the soul, and the spirit and soul would use the body as the means of expression."³

 **When Jesus controls our thoughts, choices, and feelings, He is ruling.**

We can think unkind thoughts that are clearly not godly and we can receive life-giving revelation from the Holy Spirit. We can, and often do, make bad choices; while, on the other hand, we can obey God. We can feel carnal emotions and we can experience the fruit of the Spirit. Jesus gave us His peace as a gift so it is always available for us when we are in His presence (see John 14:27). Therefore, our soul consists of our mind, will, and emotions and each faculty can be under the influence of flesh or spirit (either the Holy Spirit or evil spirits).

Since God created each one of us to be thinking, willing, and feeling beings, He wants to be Lord of our mind, will, and emotions. Throughout the Bible we're told God's thoughts are higher than our thoughts (see Isaiah 55:8-9; Romans 11:33-34), His will is preferable to the choices we would make on our own (see Proverbs 14:12; 3:5-7), and His love is superior to our negative emotions or selfish desires (see 1 Corinthians 13; 1 John 2:15-17).

God wants to be the Lord of our *entire* life, not just our "spiritual" life. Jesus said, *"God is Spirit, and those who worship Him must worship in spirit and truth"* (John 4:24). Jesus not only tells us that God is a Spirit, but that He is also known and worshiped through the spirit—our human spirit. In other words, a spiritual God communicates with humans in the realm of the spirit. There is no other way to know God than by the Spirit of God revealing Himself to our human spirit. This is why Paul writes to the Corinthians, reminding them:

> *But God has revealed them to us through His Spirit. For the Spirit searches all things, yes, the deep things of God. For what man knows the things of a man except the spirit of the man which is in him? Even so no one knows*

the things of God except the Spirit of God. Now we have received, not the spirit of the world, but the Spirit who is from God, that we might know the things that have been freely given to us by God (1 Corinthians 2:10-12).

 **A spiritual God communicates with humans in the realm of the spirit.**

AN EMOTIONAL GOD

The Scriptures reveal that God has emotions—He gives and receives love, He laughs and cries, He is pleased and angered. He not only has emotions, but His very nature is emotional. God doesn't have carnal emotions like human beings, however. His emotions are infinitely pure and holy. Apostle John writes, *"...God is love, and he who abides in love abides in God, and God in him"* (1 John 4:16). God does not simply possess love—He *is* love. His very nature is love. Before the Fall, the entire atmosphere of the Garden of Eden was permeated with the love, joy, and peace of God—the emotions of God.

Our emotions were created to be *conduits* of God's supernatural emotions. Likewise, our thoughts should be transmitters of God's thoughts and our will should agree with God's will when we are aligned properly with the Lord.

 **Our emotions were created to be conduits of God's emotions.**

PERFECT HARMONY

Before Adam and Eve sinned, they were in perfect harmony with God's thoughts, will, and emotions. In fact, they were created to be *transmitters* of His emotions, which we know now as the *"fruit of the Spirit"* (Galatian 5:22-23).

> *Beloved, let us love one another, for love is of God; and everyone who loves is born of God and knows God* (1 John 4:7).

However, once sin entered the world, their spirits were separated from God—they died a spiritual death at the very moment they ate of the fruit of the tree of knowledge of good and evil. Harmony between God and man was suddenly fractured. Adam and Eve became ruled by the flesh rather than by their spirit. Their fallen nature and God's heavenly nature no longer matched.

Even though Adam had once enjoyed perfect fellowship with God before sin entered the picture, to his dismay, he now began to feel unpleasant emotions like anger—anger because Eve gave in to temptation that caused the break in relationship with God—as well as guilt, shame, and fear. The thoughts, choices, and emotions of Adam and Eve—their souls—were now under the influence of the law of sin and death. Adam and Eve suddenly felt the need to run from God when He drew near to them.

SPIRITUAL REBIRTH

When a person is born again, the capacity to commune with God is restored. Our Father is a Spirit with heavenly DNA, and His new-creation children are *spiritual* beings also. Our heavenly Father is the Father of spiritual children. He is the *"Father of spirits"* (Hebrews 12:9).

Jesus died on the cross to pay the penalty for the sins of humankind through the shedding of His own blood. He *"made peace through the blood of His cross"* (Colossians 1:20). Because of the death, burial, and resurrection of Jesus, we can experience spiritual rebirth and enjoy communion with God once again.

 **When we are born again, our capacity to commune with God is restored.**

Christians, then, find themselves in a battle between flesh and Spirit. When a person is saved, his or her human spirit is made alive, but the carnal nature wars against the Spirit within. Have you ever tried to mix oil and water? Both are liquids, but each is a very different substance. Molecules of oil are attracted to each other but are repelled by water molecules. In the same way, our flesh and spirit repel one another. Oil doesn't intermingle with water and flesh can't connect with spirit. Paul says, *"For the flesh lusts against the Spirit, and the Spirit against the flesh; and these are contrary to one another, so that you do not do the things that you wish"* (Galatians 5:17).

If we are flesh-ruled, our life is sub-human. However, when we are Spirit-ruled we are living the normal Christian life. Our spirit, not our flesh, rules our soul when Jesus is ruling. That is how God designed us to live.

Endnotes

1. Craig von Buseck, "What Are the Three Parts of Man," *Christian Broadcast Network*, Spiritual Life; http://www1.cbn.com/questions/what-are-the-three-parts-of-man, accessed October 16, 2018.
2. Watchman Nee, *The Release of the Spirit* (Cleveland, OH: Sure Foundation Publishers, 1965), 6.
3. Ibid.

Chapter 3

CREATED FOR RELATIONSHIP

The Lord began to bring order to the darkness and chaos of Jason's life, just as He had at the time of creation. It was truly a new beginning for Jason. One of the most significant ways God transformed Jason's life was through his relationships—with both God and people. We were created for communion and community: *"It is not good that man should be alone..."* (Genesis 2:18).

IN THE BEGINNING

The sun shone brightly on the sparkling water teeming with fish and other marine life. Birds of all kinds filled the sky and the Garden was lush with plant life. Reptiles, mammals, and buzzing insects roamed the earth. It was the final day of creation. As Father God surveyed His handiwork, He declared that all was good. The stage was set for the masterpiece of God's creation. One final act was necessary for perfection: *"God created man in His own image, in the image of God He created him; male and female He created them"* (Genesis 1:27 NASB). God's crowning glory was a man and woman created in God's image (see Psalm 8:4-6; Hebrews 2:7).

 *We are God's crowning glory.*

From the very beginning, God's beloved son and daughter were fashioned in the image of God so they could have fellowship with Him. Father God made Adam and Eve to be members of His family. They weren't robots or slaves but beings with a free will so they could choose or reject having relationship with God.

> When God created Adam and Eve, He prepared a special home for them in...the Garden of Eden, where God made every provision available to them.... God created Eden to be a place of pleasure; a place of peace, tranquility and safety, a place where one could enjoy the kind of lifestyle which most people today can only dream of. Within Eden was a garden, a special place where they would meet and fellowship with God, enjoying an intimate relationship. Knowing the Lord was to be a pleasurable and very personal experience.[1]

Relationship with God

According to the Scriptures, God's design for us has always included relationship with Him. Did the Lord design humans with the unique ability to seek and discover Him? It seems that He did. In almost all societies, primitive or modern, people reflect upon the existence of God, seemingly drawn to the concept of a spiritual realm.

Throughout the history of the world, every major civilization has embraced some form of religion.[2] In the United States today, 89 percent of the population believe God exists.[3] The Pew

Research Center found that more than 80 percent of all people worldwide identify with a religious group.[4] Apparently, we are created to seek God.

God's design includes relationship with Him.

What is inside us, in the way we are fashioned, that causes us to search for God? We were made with needs that cause us to search for something to meet each need. We seek food when we are hungry. We seek water when we are thirsty. We seek social connections for relationship. We seek happiness because we sense our emptiness. However, when self seeks to satisfy self with self, we find ourselves disillusioned. As King Solomon lamented late in his life, *"I have seen all the works that are done under the sun; and indeed, all is vanity* [empty, meaningless] *and grasping for the wind"* (Ecclesiastes 1:14).

As believers, we understand that the only way we can truly find satisfaction and contentment lies in discovering that which fills our greatest need—God Himself. Blaise Pascal (1623–1662), French mathematician, physicist, inventor, and Christian philosopher, writes:

> What…does this craving…proclaim but that there was once in man a true happiness, of which all that now remains is the empty print and trace? This he tries in vain to fill with everything around him, seeking in things that are not there the help he cannot find in those that are, though none can help, since this infinite

abyss can be filled only with an infinite and immutable object; in other words by God Himself.⁵

BORN TO BELIEVE

We are born to believe. We seek God because we were *created* to need Him. Furthermore, the Lord made us with the capacity to *find* Him: *"You will seek Me and find Me, when you search for Me with all your heart. I will be found by you..."* (Jeremiah 29:13-14). And: *"When You said, 'Seek My face,' my heart said to You, 'Your face, Lord, I will seek'"* (Psalm 27:8).

Dr. Andrew Newberg, medical doctor and neuroscientist, has researched the relationship between brain functions and various mental states and has pioneered a field of research called *neurotheology*, which studies how the brain responds to and perceives religious and spiritual experiences. He hypothesizes that human beings throughout the ages have sought God because He has equipped us with "transcendent machinery" so we can discover Him.⁶

God has equipped us to discover Him.

EMOTIONS AND SPIRITUAL EXPERIENCE

The emotional center of the brain, the limbic system, is very active in spiritual experience. It appears that emotions are essential in religion and spirituality. While it is true that we need mental understanding, head and heart must function together to make sense of religious perceptions. Scientists studying the neuroscience of spiritual experience have found that all genuine spiritual experience profoundly impacts the emotions.

> Studies have also indicated that the limbic system [the center of emotional perception in the brain] is integral to religious and spiritual experiences.... Because of its involvement in religious and spiritual experiences, the limbic system has sometimes been referred to as the "transmitter to God."[7]

NEUROSCIENCE AND SPIRITUAL EXPERIENCE

It appears that four particular areas in the brain are keys to the spiritual potential of the mind. Three of these areas show *heightened activity* in brain scans of individuals during times of intense prayer. Those particular centers are responsible for processing visual imagery, abstract concepts, and focused attention. Therefore, we would logically expect these results when studying spirituality and brain activity.

The big surprise was the discovery that one part of the brain showed *decreased* activity in brain scans. A key area in the brain that defines "self" (the orientation association area, or OAA) shows significantly diminished brain activity during intense prayer. When we pray, God increases but *self* decreases! *"He must increase, but I must decrease"* (John 3:30).

> We know that the orientation area never rests, so what could account for this unusual drop in activity levels in this small section of the brain? As we pondered the question, a fascinating possibility emerged. What if the

orientation area was working as hard as ever, but the incoming flow of sensory information had somehow been blocked? That would explain the drop in brain activity in the region. More compellingly, it would also mean that the OAA had been temporarily "blinded," deprived of the information it needed to do its job properly.[8]

 God increases as self decreases.

Science has now verified that we are made with the "equipment" to seek God and find Him.[9] It appears that our brain has ability to function as a bridge joining head and heart together in spiritual experience.[10] "Science has surprised us, and our research has left us no choice but to conclude...that the mind's machinery of transcendence may in fact be a window through which we can glimpse the ultimate realness of something that is truly divine."[11] Our encounters with God are biologically, observably, and measurably real!

> The mind remembers mystical experience with the same degree of clarity and sense of reality that it bestows upon memories of "real" past events. The same cannot be said of hallucinations, delusions, or dreams. We believe this sense of realness strongly suggests that the accounts of the mystics [those who have deep experiences with God] are not indications of minds in disarray, but are the proper, predictable neurological

result of a stable, coherent mind willing itself to a higher spiritual plane.[12]

In prayer, our spirit overrides our normal self-awareness.

RELATIONSHIPS WITH PEOPLE

We not only need God, we need other people. God pronounced all of His creation good. However, after He formed Adam, He announced that one thing was *not* good, *"It is not good for the man to be alone, so I will create a companion for him, a perfectly suited partner"* (Genesis 2:18 The VOICE Bible). The remedy God provided was Eve, a woman taken from Adam's side to be his partner and companion.

Social connection defines humanity. Dr. John Cacioppo, in his book *Loneliness: Human Nature and the Need for Social Connection,* demonstrates the importance of community in human life. As the old song goes, people really do need people.

It appears, however, that what matters is not quantity but *quality*—it's not the number of social connections but "the degree to which social interactions satisfied the individual's specific, subjective need for connection."[13] "What [predicted] loneliness was... an issue of quality: the individuals' ratings of the meaningfulness, or the meaninglessness, of their encounters with other people."[14]

Social connection defines humanity.

Human beings were not meant to live in isolation. Emotional connections bond parents and infants together. The emotional information transmitted by parents stabilizes, regulates, and maintains both the physical and emotional health of the infant. This information balances hormone levels, heart function, sleep rhythms, and functioning of the immune system.

As a matter of fact, all humans benefit from staying in sync with others throughout their lives for biological equilibrium as well as satisfying the need for companionship. Human society and physiology are interdependent. Studies indicate that those who attend church regularly and engage in religious practices such as having a regular prayer life, enjoying fellowship with other believers, and engaging in charitable activities have better physical, mental, and emotional health[15] than the non-religious or those who rarely or never go to church.

THE SOCIAL BRAIN

Over the past few decades, knowledge about how the brain operates has exploded. Research about the brain has captivated the imagination of its modern-day audience.

> Why do humans do what they do? What makes us tick? With increasingly sophisticated technology, experts can image, manipulate, and scientifically test the human experience to a depth never before realized. Will this technology give us better insight into why we make the decisions we do? Can it help us understand the nature of spiritual experiences? How will understanding the brain affect our self-perception? ...

Understanding how all of this occurs is a fascinating challenge.[16]

In 1997, Gordon Shulman, Research Professor of Neurology at Washington University School of Medicine, and his colleagues published two highly significant papers on the location of physiological processes in the brain. In one of them, Shulman asked, "What does our brain do when we are doing nothing?" And: "What regions of the brain are 'more active when people were at rest, doing nothing, than when they were performing any of the specific tasks.'"[17] They called these interconnected brain structures the *default mode network*.

> [T]he default mode network is a group of brain regions that seem to show lower levels of activity when we are engaged in a particular task like paying attention, but higher levels of activity when we are awake and not involved in any specific mental exercise. It is during these times that we might be daydreaming, recalling memories, envisioning the future, monitoring the environment, thinking about the intentions of others, and so on—all things that we often do when we find ourselves just "thinking" without any explicit goal of thinking in mind.[18]

Amazingly, it appears that this particular network focuses entirely on social information. Our brain itself is wired for relationship. Whenever we are not actively engaged in a task, including all rest or free time, the brain zeroes in on other people, relationships, and ourselves.

When the brain is not focused on a specific task, when there are no tax spreadsheets or art inventories to be updated, the brain turns to its lifelong passion. What is it that the human brain likes to practice? Clearly it must be extremely important to our success and well-being in life. The brain...[was not designed] to spend its free time practicing something irrelevant to our lives. Indeed, the discovery that the brain is constantly practicing something...[says a lot] about the value of that particular thing.[19]

 **Our brain is wired for relationship.**

We automatically focus on people, relationships, ourselves, or God whenever we aren't busy. Our brain is programmed to direct our attention to the social world.[20] "It is the brain's preferred state of being, one that it returns to literally the second it has a chance."[21] Since social acceptance is the main focus of brain activity, it is not surprising that rejection is one of our greatest fears.

The Scriptures said all along that we are created to be relational beings. Now science is catching up with the Bible. It is abundantly clear that we are both spiritually *and* physiologically fashioned for relationship.

Endnotes

1. Orlando Figueiredo, "Created in God's Image," Global Word Ministry, 2012; https://www.globalwordministry.org/creation/created-in-god-s-image/, accessed October 9, 2018.

2. Joshua J. Mark, "Religion in the Ancient World," *Ancient History Encyclopedia*, March 23, 2018; https://www.ancient.eu/religion/, accessed October 8, 2018.
3. Frank Newport, "Most Americans Still Believe in God," Gallup (June 29, 2016); http://www.gallup.com/poll/193271/americans-believe-God.aspx, accessed October 8, 2018."The Global Religious Landscape," Pew Research Center, Religion and Public Life (December 18, 2012); http://www.pewforum.org/2012/12/18/global-religious-landscape-exec/, accessed September 8, 2013.Blaise Pascal, *Les Pensees* (New York: Penguin Books, 1966), 75.
4. Andrew Newberg, Eugene d'Aquili, and Vince Rause, *Why God Won't Go Away: Brain Science and the Biology of Belief* (New York: Ballantine Books, Random House Publishing Group, 2001), 8, 140-141.
5. Ibid., 42-43.
6. Ibid., 4-6.
7. Ibid., 113, 174.
8. Humans are spirit beings who have souls (thoughts, will, and emotions) and live in bodies. (Animals consist of only soul and body.) God has given us the capacity to interact with the realm of the spirit and discover Him. When we are born again, our spirit is made alive unto God and can then touch God's Spirit. Unsaved individuals also have spirits, but their spirits are "dead," or separated from God. Both believer and nonbeliever can have spiritual experiences. The question is, what spiritual realm is contacted—evil or Holy?
9. For those seeking deep spiritual experience, or "transcendent states," there is a primary difference between *how* they seek and *what* they seek. Scientists have studied both Christians and non-Christians, people of all types of religious persuasions, and found

the neural evidence of spiritual experience is very similar (when studied on brain scans). It should not be surprising that our spiritual capacity can be used both for good and evil. However, when we come to God, we come in faith believing that we can safely open our heart to Him: *"If a son asks for bread from any father among you, will he give him a stone? Or if he asks for a fish, will he give him a serpent instead of a fish? Or if he asks for an egg, will he offer him a scorpion? If you then, being evil, know how to give good gifts to your children, how much more will your heavenly Father give the Holy Spirit to those who ask Him!"* (Luke 11:11-13).

10. Newberg, *Why God Won't Go Away*, 140-141.
11. Ibid., 6-7, 113, 174.
12. John Cacioppo and William Patrick, *Loneliness: Human Nature and the Need for Social Connection* (New York, NY: W.W. Norton & Company, 2008), 94.
13. Ladd Wheeler, Harry Reis, and John B. Nezlek, "Loneliness, Social Interaction, and Sex Roles," *Journal of Personality and Social Psychology*, 45 (1983), 943-953.
14. Harold Koenig and Malcolm McConnell, *The Healing Power of Faith* (New York: Simon and Schuster, 2001), 258; Jeffrey S. Levin, "Religion and Health: Is There an Association, Is It Valid, and Is It Causal?" *Social Science Medicine*, Vol. 38, No. 11 (1994), 1475-1482.
15. "Neuroscience, Brain, and Mind," American Association of the Advancement of Science; https://www.aaas.org/programs/dialogue-science-ethics-and-religion/neuroscience-brain-mind, accessed October 16, 2018.
16. Gordon Shulman, Maurizzio Corbetta, Randy Lee Buckner, Julie A. Fiez, Francis M. Miezin, Marcus E. Raichle, and Steven E. Petersen, "Common Blood Flow Changes across Visual Tasks:

I. Increases in Subcortical Structures and Cerebellum but Not in Nonvisual Cortex," *Journal of Cognitive Neuroscience*, 9(5), (1997), 624-647.
17. Gordon Shulman, Julie A. Fiez, Maurizzio Corbetta, Randy Lee Buckner, Francis M. Miezin, Marcus E. Raichle, and Steven E. Petersen, "Common Blood Flow Changes across Visual Tasks: II. Decreases in Cerebral Cortex," *Journal of Cognitive Neuroscience*, 15(3), (1997), 648-663.
18. "Know Your Brain: Default Mode Network," Neuroscientifically Challenged (June 16, 2015); https://www.neuroscientificallychallenged.com/blog/know-your-brain-default-mode-network.
19. Matthew D. Lieberman, *Social: Why Our Brains Are Wired to Connect* (New York: Crown Publishing Group, 2013), 15.
20. Robert P. Spunt, Megan L. Meyer and Matthew D. Lieberman, "Social by Default: Brain Activity at Rest Facilitates Social Cognition," *Journal of Cognitive Neuroscience*, V. 27, (6), (June 2015), 1116-1124; Randy L. Buckner, Jessica R. Andrews-Hanna, and Daniel L. Schacter, "The Brain's Default Network," *Annals of the New York Academy of Sciences* ,1124(1), (2008), 1-38.
21. Lieberman, *Social*, 21.

Chapter 4

WHAT IS A SOUL TIE?

Soul ties are emotional bonds that form an attachment. They may be godly or ungodly, pure or demonic. Most people use the term *soul tie* to refer to connections linking people. Soul ties are not necessarily sexual or romantic. It is not uncommon for individuals to form attachments with counselors, physicians, coworkers, teachers, or even celebrities they have never met.

 **Soul ties are emotional bonds that form an attachment.**

However, contrary to what is commonly believed, soul ties are not always links between individuals. We can form an ungodly attachment with any person, place, or thing. Individuals can be overly attached to pets, possessions, or anything else imaginable: *"...You are a slave to whatever controls you"* (2 Peter 2:19 NLT).

> *They traded the truth about God for a lie. So they worshiped and served the things God created instead of the Creator himself, who is worthy of eternal praise!* (Romans 1:25 NLT)

The Will of God

We are created to need an intimate relationship with God and are truly fulfilled when we are in union with Him. Any desire or love that hinders us from doing the will of God is an inordinate, or lustful, affection. When our soul functions as God intended, we are submitted to Him spirit, soul, and body. We then experience the peace of His presence and abide in Him.[1]

> *I am the vine, you are the branches. He who abides in Me, and I in him, bears much fruit; for without Me you can do nothing* (John 15:5).

Jesus, our pattern, "made a decision to be controlled only by God, and no one else, even those whom He greatly loved. We must do the same, determining not to allow even loving relationships such as family or friends to draw us into a state of disobedience to God. Anything less than full, total and immediate obedience is disobedience."[2]

 **Anything less than full, total, and immediate obedience is disobedience.**

Refusing to be in bondage to family and friends, Jesus never submitted to selfish desires or tried to prove Himself to man. Jesus also rejected the pressure of the devil in the wilderness. First, Jesus was tempted in His body: *He was hungry but refused to use His divine power for Himself* (see Luke 4:2-4).

Next, Jesus was tempted in His *soul* to validate His own identity and function apart from His Father's timetable:

> *Then the devil took Him up into the holy city, set Him on the pinnacle of the temple, and said to Him, "**If You are the Son of God**, throw Yourself down. For it is written: 'He shall give His angels charge over you,' and, 'In their hands they shall bear you up, lest you dash your foot against a stone.'" Jesus said to him, "It is written again, 'You shall not tempt the Lord your God'"* (Matthew 4:5-7).

Finally, Jesus was tempted in His *Spirit* to do the will of the devil rather than the will of the Father. By giving in to selfish desires, we worship self and thereby worship the devil:

> *Again, the devil took Him up on an exceedingly high mountain, and showed Him all the kingdoms of the world and their glory. And he said to Him, "**All these things I will give You if You will fall down and worship me**." Then Jesus said to him, "Away with you, Satan! For it is written, 'You shall worship the Lord your God, and Him only you shall serve." Then the devil left Him, and behold, angels came and ministered to Him* (Matthew 4:8-11).

Jesus declined to submit Himself to an ungodly spirit. He refused man-pleasing, self-pleasing, or acting at the behest of an evil spirit. He was in bondage to no man or devil. Finally, in the Garden of Gethsemane, Jesus refused the temptation to cling to His own life for self-preservation when He brought "His flesh into submission to His Spirit, which was already in obedience unto the will of God."[3] Instead, He exclaimed, *"Father, if it is Your will, take this cup away from Me; nevertheless not My will, but Yours, be done"* (Luke 22:42).

God doesn't want our soul in bondage to soul ties that turn our heart away from Him. "God desires to restore our soul that we might be able to seek Him with our whole (entire) spirit, soul, and body.... We cannot be obedient to God's command to serve Him with all of our soul if we lack possession of a complete, whole soul![4] *"Now may the God of peace Himself sanctify you completely; and may your whole **spirit, soul,** and **body** be preserved blameless at the coming of our Lord Jesus Christ"* (1 Thessalonians 5:23).

 *God doesn't want our soul in bondage to soul ties.*

Above all else, we are called to be in union with God and be yoked together with Him. *"**Take My yoke** upon you and learn from Me, for I am gentle and lowly in heart, and **you will find rest for your souls**"* (Matthew 11:29). If our soul is bound by an ungodly soul tie, it has departed from commitment to God and linked itself to another influence.

Just as a baby is joined with his or her mother by the umbilical cord, Jesus uses the analogy of a vine and branches to illustrate our vital connection with Him. He is the True Vine and we are branches joined to Him for supernatural life, sustenance, strength, and fruit bearing. We must not only be *obedient* to God but should be completely *dependent* upon Him as well. Jesus says in John 5:19, *"Most assuredly, I say to you, **the Son can do nothing of Himself**, but what He sees the Father do; for whatever He does, the Son also does in like manner."* Likewise, He tells us, *"**Abide in**

*Me, and I in you. As the branch cannot bear fruit of itself, unless it abides in the vine, neither can you, unless you abide in Me. I am the vine, you are the branches. He who abides in Me, and I in him, bears much fruit; for **without Me you can do nothing**"* (John 15:4-5).

Soul ties may be grouped into two broad categories: (1) relational (people) or (2) idolatrous (places or things). Our primary soul tie should be union with God. He is our source and life. We were made for Him and designed to cleave unto Him. When our soul is free from ungodly bondage, we are free to serve Him with joy and perfect obedience.

RELATIONAL SOUL TIES

All relationships include emotional connections. They are made up of two individuals, and the relationship itself is a separate entity connecting the two. When relationships are ungodly, demonic activity is always involved in the form of seducing spirits. There is no middle ground with soul ties. They either glorify God or they don't. They are godly or demonic.[5] The Bible contains many warnings and guidelines about forming godly soul ties and avoiding evil ones.

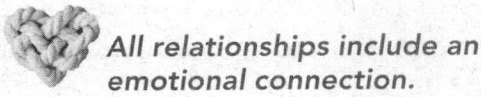

All relationships include an emotional connection.

GODLY SOUL TIES

The first godly soul tie we learn about in Scripture is the one flesh connection of marriage. Before God created Adam, He had pronounced all creation as good. However, when He made

Adam, *"The Lord God said, 'It is **not good that man should be alone**; I will make him a helper [partner] comparable to him'"* (Genesis 2:18). Adam was designed for union with his wife—his partner and companion. Although God made Adam from the dust of the ground, Eve was brought forth from Adam's side.

> *And the Lord God caused a deep sleep to fall on Adam, and he slept; and He took one of his ribs, and closed up the flesh in its place. Then the rib which the Lord God had taken from man He made into a woman, and He brought her to the man. And Adam said: "This is now bone of my bones and flesh of my flesh; she shall be called Woman, because she was taken out of Man." Therefore a man shall **leave** his father and mother and **be joined** to his wife, and **they shall become one flesh*** (Genesis 2:21-24).

This soul tie was man and wife joined together as a couple and made one flesh in sexual union. They were told to leave parents, break the emotional control, and come together in the bond of a new, godly soul tie. When we are born again, we become a new creation in Christ. Husband and wife also become a new creation in marriage—a single entity formed from two individuals joined together spirit, soul, and body. Notice the sequence of marriage as designed by God. Adam and Eve were married by God in a *spiritual* covenant. Their *souls* were knit for companionship. Finally, sexual union joined their *bodies* with one another in a union blessed by God.

 **We become a new creation in marriage.**

From this husband-wife union, they would produce children also made in the image of God and become a family unit. They were one with each other and one with God: *"And a threefold cord is not quickly broken"* (Ecclesiastes 4:12). However, breaking that cord is exactly what the enemy attempted to do. Satan immediately plotted to destroy their union with God and interfere with the first godly soul tie because of the enormous potential found in unity.

The relationship of Jonathan and David is a familiar example from the Bible of a godly soul tie of friendship: *"...the soul of Jonathan was knit to the soul of David, and Jonathan loved him as his own soul"* (1 Samuel 18:1). They entered into a covenant relationship in which Jonathan protected David from Saul's anger and also led David to tenderly care for the son of Jonathan after his death.

Love links believers together in the body of Christ through healthy, mutual friendships in which individuals are *"knit together by strong ties of love"* (Colossians 2:2 NLT). Mutual submission unites believers in fellowship and purpose: *"For where two or three are gathered together in My name, there am I [Jesus] in the midst of them"* (Matthew 18:20 KJV).

UNGODLY SOUL TIES

Soul ties, both godly and ungodly, can form with anyone including parents, siblings, friends, acquaintances, and those with whom we fellowship in church. Sexual activity is one way soul ties form in marriage and out of marriage, but the most common way is by spending time in someone's company: *"Can two walk together, unless they are agreed?"* (Amos 3:3). Agreement can produce a rescue mission or a lynch mob.

We must guard ourselves so we don't open our heart to the wrong people: *"Do not be so deceived and misled! Evil companionships (communion, associations) corrupt and deprave good manners and morals and character"* (1 Corinthians 15:33 AMPC). And: *"Do not be unequally yoked together with unbelievers. For what fellowship has righteousness with lawlessness? And what communion has light with darkness?"* (2 Corinthians 6:14).

> How do demons enter into soul ties? Evil spirits are able to enter when spiritual boundaries are violated. God has set boundaries that govern our relationships with others.... [T]here are protective boundaries set by God for marriage. A man is to forsake all others and be joined to his wife. There are similar limitations that govern friendships and bonds within the body of Christ. When relationships within any given area disregard the boundaries that God has established, the relationships become perverse and demons enter. In other words, fleshly soul ties become demonic soul ties.
>
> Through soul ties, a spiritual channel is formed. For example, in a godly marriage, the Holy Spirit flows between husband and wife.... The same principle operates in demonic soul ties. When there is a sinful joining of two individuals, demon spirits in one person open up the other person for similar spirits.[6]

 We must guard ourselves so we don't open our heart to the wrong people.

UNGODLY SOUL TIES	
Sexual sin	Vows
Inanimate objects	Addictions
Animals	Religion
Places	Unnatural grief
Secret organizations	Perverted family tie
Pornography	Music

How Ungodly Soul Ties Form

The bad choices we make concerning companionship bring us into bondage through the soul ties that form through agreement. Jesus came to set us free, but the bonds formed by ungodly associations take us captive. However, when we know how the devil works to enslave us, we can more effectively resist his wiles: *"Be sober, be vigilant; because your adversary the devil walks about like a roaring lion, seeking whom he may devour"* (1 Peter 5:8).

There are many ways that ungodly soul ties form, but common ways this happens include the following:

Association. We take on the characteristics of those with whom we choose to associate through the soul ties that form. If we spend time with angry, complaining people, we tend to mirror their behavior. If we hang around those engaging in sinful behavior, we become partakers of their sin.

> *Become wise by walking with the wise; hang out with fools and watch your life fall to pieces* (Proverbs 13:20 MSG).

> *But now I have written to you not to keep company with anyone named a brother, who is sexually immoral, or covetous, or an idolater, or a reviler, or a drunkard, or an extortioner—not even to eat with such a person* (1 Corinthians 5:11).

Harboring toxic emotions. Toxic emotions that linger are products of unforgiveness. We form bonds with those we hate. Our wounds and anger form ungodly soul ties that keep us in bondage until we forgive. When we forgive from the heart, we experience a supernatural transaction that sets us free and replaces negative emotions with the peace of God.

> *Then the king called in the man he had forgiven and said, "You evil servant! I forgave you that tremendous debt because you pleaded with me. Shouldn't you have mercy on your fellow servant, just as I had mercy on you?" Then the angry king sent the man to prison to be tortured until he had paid his entire debt. That's what my heavenly Father will do to you if you refuse to forgive your brothers and sisters from your heart* (Matthew 18:32-35 NLT).

Celeste, a young girl in middle school, had learned how to forgive effectively at one of our training sessions, but she had a relationship with a clique of girls who hurt her feelings regularly. It couldn't be called friendship because they enjoyed picking on her. For example, the girls would plan a party and deliberately not invite her. Celeste asked me (Dennis) about her feelings of rejection. I explained to her that she could escape from the cycle of victimhood by practicing forgiveness *while* they were being catty.

You can't throw dirt into a firehose when water is gushing from it. Celeste agreed to try it out.

> *He that believeth on me, as the scripture hath said, out of his belly shall flow rivers of living water* (John 7:38 KJV).

Not too long afterward, the girls came up to Celeste in the school cafeteria and made some unkind remarks; but Celeste allowed a river of love to flow from her heart to them at the same time. Needless to say, the words didn't hurt. But what happened next was the real testimony. Celeste told me that while she was letting love flow out, she felt the Holy Spirit prompt her to turn her head and direct her gaze to a group of girls sitting at a table nearby.

Celeste walked over and introduced herself. They happened to be Christians and became her new best friends. In breaking the soul tie with her tormentors, she was able to follow the leading of the Lord and see the healthy relationships God had provided.

Sexual sin. Seducing spirits are always involved when sexual sin is committed. That is why we are warned to flee sexual immorality. What does Jesus say about the matter? He not only condemned sexual immorality, which includes all sexual activity outside of traditional marriage, but He raised the standard to include holiness of heart:

> *You have heard that it was said, You shall not commit adultery. But I say to you that everyone who so much as looks at a woman with evil desire for her has already committed adultery with her in his **heart*** (Matthew 5:27-28 AMPC).

> *For out of the **heart** proceed evil thoughts, murders, adulteries, fornications, thefts, false witness, blasphemies. These are the things that defile a man...* (Matthew 15:19-20).

Prolonged grief. Whereas grief following the death of a loved one is natural, prolonged grief is unnatural. A soul tie can develop following the death of a loved one or friend. It is common when there is a death by suicide, it was sudden or unexpected, or there was an abortion. Normally, grief should last months to a couple of years at most.

> Sometimes a soul-tie with the dead can develop into a sort of "communion" with the dead person, feeling the person's presence, or seeing them repeatedly in dreams or visions.... It is not uncommon for demons to manifest as deceased relatives. They may masquerade as the relative to deceive, as in a séance, or to promote belief in reincarnation. Or, they may manifest during deliverance when the spirit of the relative [a familiar spirit] or ancestor has been passed down. If the curse and accountability for the sins of the ancestor can be passed down for generations, it should not surprise us to find that demons...can be passed down as well.[7]

The father of Theresa, a teenaged girl we know, died and she was heartbroken because of the great loss. A couple of years later, when we went to visit her mother, we were alarmed to hear that Theresa's "father" had started appearing to her as a ghostly being. We met with her privately and asked her to get in an attitude of prayer and think of the apparition. A seducing spirit manifested immediately and we had her receive forgiveness for giving it ground in her life. The evil spirit left and the visitations ceased.

Manipulation. Another way many soul ties form is through manipulation, which is a form of witchcraft. If a man becomes friends with someone because it's possibly a stepping stone for a promotion at work, it's ungodly. "He has an 'in' with the boss!" Using other people is always ungodly and gives legal ground to the enemy. Believers can also pray witchcraft prayers in an attempt to manipulate or control by praying for their will rather than God's will.

Pride. A soul tie with self can form due to excessive pride. Pride was the sin that turned Lucifer, an anointed cherub of God, into satan, the father of lies. The sin of pride is a preoccupation with self. When we exalt ourselves, in effect, we are saying, "I am my own god." Anything you love more than God is an idol.

> *How you are fallen from heaven, O Lucifer, son of the morning! How you are cut down to the ground, you who weakened the nations! For you have said in your heart: "I will ascend into heaven, I will exalt my throne above the stars of God; I will also sit on the mount of the congregation on the farthest sides of the north; I will ascend above the heights of the clouds, I will be like the Most High"* (Isaiah 14:12-14).

Pride is not just an emotion, it's a spirit. It is foremost in the list of the seven deadly sins. Early church fathers thought that pride severed the soul from grace, was the very essence of evil, and the basis of all other sins.

Many years ago, I (Dennis) was ministering to a man who insisted that he was "too complicated" for me to help. As he said those words, he tilted his chin up in the air. In a flash, I saw a demon of pride superimposed over his features in the form of a bald, egg-shaped head that was looking down on me. I answered him by saying, "Roots are simple. They are either rooted in God or the devil." Pride renders us unteachable. Pride will ask for help then not listen. Common statements made by individuals with a spirit of pride include: "I'm too complicated." "Even the best can't help me." "I already know that." "That might work for others but not me."

Evil attraction. Seducing spirits attract other evil spirits. Just as the Holy Spirit brings people together for divine purposes, evil spirits can also link individuals to one another. Many years ago, a pastor living in my area referred a married woman to me (Dennis) for a prayer session. She had been behaving seductively with men at church. When we met together, I was surprised to learn that she believed demonic seduction was necessary to keep her unsaved husband satisfied sexually. She didn't want deliverance. Soon afterward, a pastor from another city insisted that a single man in his church make an appointment with me because he was making women parishioners uncomfortable with overly attentive behavior. They said he felt creepy. When he came in for an appointment, he refused to pray about it even though his unclean spirits were clearly discernible.

A few months later, I attended a banquet celebrating a Christian television ministry with four hundred in attendance. I was startled and appalled when I saw the two of them being magnetically drawn together from distant corners of the banquet hall only to strike up a friendly conversation. They lived in two different cities and had never met. Their seducing spirits drew them together.

Likewise, sexual molestation and abuse bind the victim to seducing spirits that attract other abusers to them. I (Jennifer) had a prayer appointment with an attractive college-age woman who was concerned because lesbians on campus made passes at her even though she was only interested in men. When we prayed about it, an incident from her childhood flashed in her mind. A female babysitter had sexually molested her. As soon as she pictured the incident, a seducing spirit manifested. She forgave the babysitter, broke the soul tie, surrendered her emotions back to God, and the evil spirit lifted. Women never made inappropriate advances toward her again.

Agendas. If there is something we want and we can't let it go, we bind to ourselves a seducing spirit of lust that functions as an invisible umbilical cord seeking an attachment. Unfortunately, even if we get what we want, a bad outcome is practically guaranteed.

A lovely single mother insisted that she had to have a father for her young son. We encouraged her to trust and seek God rather than looking for a man. She just couldn't let it go, however. It seems that she decided that the next single man who knocked at her door would be the one. A good-looking young man did come to her door and he moved in with her. Unfortunately, he was on medication for psychosis and believed he was Jesus. It didn't end well and she eventually lost custody of her son.

Secrecy and gossip. A bond of secrecy creates a web of darkness. "I'll tell you something but you can't tell anyone else." It binds you together with another individual and shuts others out. If the secret itself is gossip, you share in the sin of the one who gossips. Before someone shares gossip with you, they test your spirit to see if you are open. The tingle of anticipation you feel in your gut is a seducing spirit wooing you to open your heart to listen. If you listen, you're hooked. To get free, receive forgiveness, repent, and bring the secret into the light in an appropriate manner: *"If we walk in the light as He is in the light, we have fellowship with one another, and the blood of Jesus Christ His Son cleanses us from all sin"* (1 John 1:7).

IDOLATROUS SOUL TIES

Soul ties are always formed when we lust for any person, place, or thing. We usually think of lust in terms of sexual desire but lust is what makes an idol an idol. Anything we desire more than God is an idol. If we can't say, "I choose Your will over the thing I want," then we have an idol and the emotion attaching us to what we want is lust. If your vision or dream doesn't begin with God and end in God, it's an idol.

A young woman insisted on buying a house at the beach. She justified her decision according to her interpretation of Psalm 37:4, *"God will give you the desires of your heart."* However, she ignored the first part of the verse: *"Delight yourself also in the Lord."* If we delight ourselves in the Lord, He puts *His* desires in our heart and that's what He gives us.

> *But seek first the kingdom of God and His righteousness, and all these things shall be added to you* (Matthew 6:33).

She got the house she wanted and found a job but couldn't locate a church that she liked and didn't make any close friends.

Moreover, she could no longer feel the presence of God. If we insist on having our way rather than seeking God's will, we become like the children of Israel in the wilderness: *"They soon forgot His works; they did not wait for His counsel, but lusted exceedingly in the wilderness, and tested God in the desert. And He gave them their request, but sent leanness into their soul"* (Psalm 106:13-15).

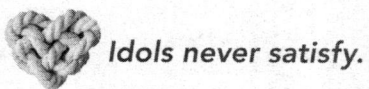 Idols never satisfy.

ENDNOTES

1. If you would like to learn more about God's will and living in peace as a lifestyle, which is evidence of abiding in Christ, our book *Flowing in the River of God's Will* covers the topic thoroughly. You can purchase it on our website at www.forgive123.com and bookstores everywhere.
2. Bill and Susan Banks, *Breaking Unhealthy Soul-Ties* (Kirkwood, MO: Impact Christian Books, 1999, 2011), 20-21.
3. Ibid., 23.
4. Ibid., 24.
5. Dephne Madyara, *Breaking Soul Ties: The Deliverance Manual* (Sutton, UK: CreateSpace Independent Publishing Platform, 2016), 20.
6. Frank Hammond, *Soul Ties* (Kirkwood, MO: Impact Christian Books, 1988, 1995, 2011), 13.
7. Banks, *Breaking Unhealthy Soul-Ties*, 98-99.

Chapter 5

THE TANGLED WEB OF CODEPENDENCY

JASON'S STORY

My relationship with Lana had only been the latest in a long series of codependent entanglements. For the previous twenty years, I had been backslidden and went from one unhealthy relationship to another. Part of the problem was that I was angry with my dad and angry at God. Another part of the problem was that, having been raised as a preacher's kid, I knew better and struggled with guilt and shame.

I later learned that I was a "needy" codependent because I didn't feel like I could make it through life alone. In addition, playing the role of a rescuer gave me a sense of purpose. Looking back, it's obvious that only God could have met my needs adequately but I avoided Him with great determination.

For My people have committed two evils: they have forsaken Me, the fountain of living waters, and hewn themselves cisterns—broken cisterns that can hold no water (Jeremiah 2:13).

Codependency

The term "codependency" is a fancy, psychological term for someone who is an extreme people-pleaser. Of course, people-pleasing runs the gamut from occasional manipulation to the avoidance of rocking the boat as a way of life.

The art of pleasing is the art of deceiving.
–French Proverb

Are you concerned about what other people think of you? Do you often make decisions based on what you think will please others? Does your sense of self-worth come from the approval of others? Do you often withhold from sharing what you truly want, think or feel because of fear it may upset someone? Are you often last on your list of priorities?[1]

Codependency is a psychological term for a common behavioral pattern—people-pleasing. However, when manipulative people-pleasing becomes the basis of a relationship it undermines. Rather than being a mental health diagnosis, codependency is a cluster of behavioral patterns. It is a relationship addiction because codependents commonly gravitate toward one-sided relationships that are harmful and sometimes abusive. They use others in an attempt to get their emotional needs met in a way that is selfish and destructive.

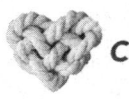 **Codependency is a relationship addiction.**

Trust is the foundation for all relationships with God and with people. Codependents are afraid to trust others, including God, so they feel that they can only trust themselves. Without trust, emotional isolation is guaranteed. Codependents are often extremely anxious at the prospect of true intimacy with other people, so an unhealthy relationship helps them avoid being *alone* while maintaining a comfortable emotional distance. A codependent person substitutes activities for intimacy.

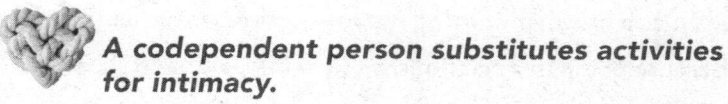

A codependent person substitutes activities for intimacy.

Relationship types. Individuals with codependency often form or maintain relationships that are one-sided. Two common examples of codependent relationships are rescuer-victim and caretaker-dependent. They try to make the relationship work with someone who doesn't make an effort.

Denial. The parties involved in a dysfunctional relationship generally refuse to acknowledge existing issues because they are in denial. Because codependents don't trust, they fail to talk about problems or deal with them. At the same time, they disregard their own feelings and personal needs. However, not all caring behavior and sympathetic feelings indicate codependency—only those that are excessive and unhealthy.

Codependents are fixated on the *needs* or *control* of another person. They may seem to be either clingy and needy or competent and controlling while enabling the harmful behaviors of their partner to continue unchallenged.

CODEPENDENTS ARE DEPENDENT ON THE NEEDS OR CONTROL OF ANOTHER.

Needy Codependents

Codependents often lose contact with their sense of self and put the needs of others before their own. They "need to be needed" so much that they can't bear the thought of not having someone need them. Caring for others does not come from love and compassion. It is a manipulative tool they use to get their own needs met while maintaining the connection with their partner.

Because being in a relationship is so important to them, codependents may alternate between "smothering" their partner with their caretaking, then getting angry because they have put so much responsibility on themselves, or becoming emotionally distraught when the balance of the relationship is disturbed (if they think their partner is interested in someone else or become afraid their partner might leave them).

Codependent individuals derive fulfillment by attempting to manage the emotions and behaviors of their partner while neglecting themselves. They get their satisfaction through their "need to be needed" instead of enjoying true intimacy with another person. An example of this would be when one person does everything to try to make the relationship work while their partner contributes little.

Codependent individuals try to manage other people's emotions and behaviors but neglect themselves.

Controlling Codependents

Although some codependents seem obviously needy, others act like they're self-sufficient and responsible. The self-sufficient codependent's *need* is to find their sense of purpose in life by becoming a "savior" to someone else. Because codependents *need* their partner to behave in a particular way so they can feel good about themselves, they feel the need to *control* any person who is close to them. When they are in control, they feel safe and secure.

Rescuing gives the codependent individual a sense of being valuable and competent. At the same time, they consider themselves to be superior to their partner and are secretly proud of their role as a rescuer or caretaker. They can be the "better person," "the smarter person," or the "person who seems to have it all together."

Characteristics of Codependency

Codependency may include excessive caretaking, a sense of unworthiness, people-pleasing behaviors, control, denial, and manipulation. It is commonly characterized by the following symptoms:

- Trying to solve other people's problems
- Feeling overly responsible for others
- Trying to control the feelings of others
- Only feeling "safe" when doing or giving to others
- Feeling guilty when others *give* to them or *do* for them
- Accepting abuse or being used to avoid being alone
- Having a pattern of unhealthy relationships

QUESTIONS TO ASK

If you are wondering if you are in a codependent relationship, ask yourself the following questions:

- Is this relationship more important to me than I am?
- Do I feel like I can't survive without them?
- Do I feel like they won't survive without me?
- What price am I paying for being in this relationship?
- Am I the only one putting energy into the relationship?

COUNTERDEPENDENCY

Those who suffer [from] counterdependency have a dread of ever depending on or needing anyone, at the heart of which is an inability to trust. If there was...[an underlying belief] that all counterdependents have, it would probably be "I don't need anyone."

Counterdependents can often come across as vibrant, 'life of the party' sorts...[and] have many friends and relationships. The difference is that those relationships will not be deep and trusting, and might not last. So one of the main signs of counterdependency is an inability to have connected and authentic relationships.... A counterdependent person will initially be attracted to the codependent's apparent show of understanding and warmth...because underneath a counterdependent person's belief they don't need anyone is a deep desire to finally be able to let their guard down and fully trust and love another.

Because codependency and counterdependency both revolve around needing others, whether that is wanting or avoiding, it's not uncommon for partners in a 'dependency based' relationship to switch roles.[2]

Developmental Disruptions

Both codependency and counterdependency are caused by developmental disruptions during infancy and early childhood. The two main lessons that need to be learned in early childhood are bonding and separation.

Bonding. Bonding occurs through the emotional attachment formed between mother and infant as the child learns trust and emotional intimacy in a safe environment. The infant needs to experience unconditional love, nurturing, and protection from a trustworthy caregiver. If these needs are not met adequately, there is insecure or incomplete bonding.

The infant brain develops within an interpersonal context, where structural and functional networks are shaped by the nature and quality of early caregiver-infant interactions. This "experience-dependent" nature of brain development has consistently been illustrated in studies of groups of children who were exposed to early aberrant, caregiving environments. For instance, early disruptions to early caregiver–child relationships have been found to result in alterations of particular brain regions implicated in emotional regulation.[3]

The bonding stage occurs during the first twelve months of life and the mother plays the primary role during this time. Neuroscientists have learned that patterns for attachment and bonding throughout life are hardwired in infancy and early childhood. Emotional needs that aren't met in infancy and early childhood result in the formation of black holes of deprivation. These unmet needs create an inner drive to successfully satisfy those needs in relationships later in life. However, codependent behavior in adulthood sabotages the likelihood of truly meeting those needs.

Attachment patterns stabilize in our neural circuity by 12-18 months of age. They are stable and unconscious before we have any conscious choice in the matter and, unless new experiences change them, will remain stable "rules" of relating well into adulthood.[4]

Our patterns of attachment are triggered automatically and are beyond our conscious control. Nevertheless, they are in continuous operation and drive our social interactions and behaviors.

Separation. Separation is the second stage that takes place from six months to 36 months. During this time children learn they can be separate individuals and still be safely attached to caregivers. Although the mother is still needed, the father's role becomes crucial during the phase of separation.

The brain circuitry for how we approach all relationships later in life develops within the first three years of life. It's like links in a chain that are available at birth but require social learning to be connected in relational patterns. Those patterns can be healthy or dysfunctional.

> During infancy, fathers have been shown to be competent and capable of similar successful interactions with young infants and to have similar psychological experiences as mothers. However, their relationship is not redundant; the father is more likely to be the infant's play partner than the mother, and father's play tends to be more stimulating, vigorous, and arousing for the infant.
>
> Fathers were equally successful in matching emotions with their children (during social interactions, fathers were able to synchronize arousal rhythms with their infants just as successfully as mothers), but the quality of interactions (especially play) was more intense with fathers. These high-intensity interactions with fathers may encourage children's exploration and independence, whereas the less-intensive interactions with mothers provide safety and balance.[5]

Counterdependency can be traced to the negativity of the two-year-old. The child needs to learn appropriate discipline without emotional, physical, or sexual abuse. Abuse disrupts their sense of safety and they learn to fear. The child puts up walls of protection when caregivers are not trustworthy. Counterdependent individuals suffer from deep fear and insecurity. Although they may long for intimacy, their emotional walls and avoidant behaviors guarantee emotional isolation. Counterdependents may seem to be strong, confident, and successful outwardly but inwardly be weak, insecure, fearful, and needy.

PATTERNS AND ROOTS

What we learn becomes linked together in our brain forming a lifelong pattern for relationships. If an infant learns rejection from his or her mother, the child will have a love deficit and will unconsciously repeat that pattern trying to get the void filled throughout life. If a child learns fear and mistrust from caregivers, he or she will hide behind walls while yearning inwardly for love.

We have two types of memory: explicit and implicit. *Explicit* memory is information stored in long- and short-term memory. We can consciously retrieve it. It is something we have learned. When information is stored in *implicit* memory, it is both unconscious and unintentional. We are not able to consciously bring it into awareness. It is just something that is "a part of us."

> Any emotional-relational-social experiences that are processed before the brain structures that can process experience consciously are fully mature, before 2½-3 years of age...are stored only in implicit memory, outside of awareness. This includes all early patterns of attachment.[6]

As adults, both codependents and counterdependents unconsciously try to complete the bonding-separation process in a satisfactory way so they get their needs met but automatically repeat the same dysfunctional patterns that guarantee failure. They consistently get involved in unhealthy relationships as a result.

Fortunately, when God heals our heart, faulty patterns of behavior are healed as well! *"When my father and my mother forsake me, then the Lord will take care of me"* (Psalm 27:10).

"For I know the plans that I have for you," declares the Lord, "plans for welfare and not for calamity, to give you a future and a hope" (Jeremiah 29:11).

IDENTIFYING ROOTS OF CODEPENDENCY AND COUNTERDEPENDENCY

Answer the following questions to identify some possible roots of *codependency*:

- What do you wish your parents (or caregivers) had done for you when you were a child?
- What did you need from them that you didn't receive?

To identify the roots of *counterdependency*, answer this question:

- What do you wish your parents or caregivers had not done or said when you were a child?

It is possible for an individual to have roots for *both* codependency and counterdependency. How can you find healing for the ache in your heart? The answers are found in the following section.

ENDNOTES

1. Christine Hassler, "Why Being a People-Pleaser is Selfish," *The Huffington Post*, (August 12, 2017); https://www.huffingtonpost.com/entry/why-being-a-people-pleaser-is-selfish_us_598fc39de4b0caa1687a60d0

2. "The Dangers of Counterdependency: When You Never Need Anyone," Harley Therapy (September 15, 2015); https://www.harleytherapy.co.uk/counselling/what-is-counterdependency.htm, accessed October 23, 2018.
3. Louise Newman, Carmel Silvaratnum, and Angela Komiti, "Attachment and Early Brain Development: Neuroprotective Interventions in Infant-Caregiver Therapy," Translational Developmental Psychiatry (May 25, 2015), 3:1, DOI: 10.3402/tdp.v3.28647; https://www.tandfonline.com/doi/full/10.3402/tdp.v3.28647
4. Linda Graham, "The Neuroscience of Attachment," Resources for Recovering Resilience (September 5, 2008). First presented as a Clinical Conversation at the Community Institute for Psychotherapy (Fall 2008); https://lindagraham-mft.net/the-neuroscience-of-attachment/, accessed October 5, 2018.
5. Michael Yogman and Craig F. Garfield, "Fathers' Roles in the Care and Development of Their Children: The Role of Pediatricians," The American Academy of Pediatrics Clinical Report (June 2016); http://pediatrics.aappublications.org/content/early/2016/06/10/peds.2016-1128, accessed October 20, 2018.
6. Graham, "The Neuroscience of Attachment."

 *Section Two*

FINDING FREEDOM

Chapter 6

SPIRITUAL ANATOMY

Many believers erroneously believe that the word "heart" in the Bible refers to the physical heart in the chest, especially because so many modern translations have substituted the generic word *heart* for the original Hebrew and Greek words. When the Bible talks about the heart of man, it refers to the "belly" or "bowels" (the actual words used in both the Hebrew Old Testament and the Greek New Testament). This doesn't mean your heart and spirit are in a physical organ of the body. It just means the belly area is the epicenter of spiritual and emotional activity.

 **The belly is the epicenter of spiritual and emotional activity.**

LOCATION OF THE HEART

In the Old Testament, the word "bowels," *me'ah* in Hebrew, is correctly translated in the King James Version of the Bible, but the less accurate word "heart" is substituted in later translations. The Hebrew word used for "heart" in the Song of Solomon 5:4 is *me'ah*, meaning "inward parts, digestive organs, bowels, womb, or, figuratively, the place of emotions of distress or love." When the Shulamite's Beloved came to her, she says, *"[M]y bowels were moved for Him,"* meaning that her heart was moved with affection.

In the New Testament, we find that the heart of man is also located in the belly. Jesus said, *"He that believeth on Me, as the scripture hath said, out of his belly shall flow rivers of living water,"* indicating that the epicenter of spiritual activity is in the belly area (John 7:38 KJV). In the original Greek, the word used here is *koilia*, meaning "belly." Later translations use the English word "heart" instead of belly, but belly is the correct translation.

Only one verse in the New Testament refers to the physical heart, Luke 21:26: *"Men's hearts failing them from fear...."* The Greek word *apopsucho* is used for "hearts failing" meaning their physical hearts "breathe out life" or they "die." With this one exception, "heart" always refers to the innermost being. According to *Vine's Expository Dictionary of Old and New Testament Words*:

> By easy transition the word [heart] came to stand for man's entire mental and moral activity, both the rational and emotional elements. In other words, the heart is used figuratively for the hidden springs of the personal life. ...Scripture regards the heart as the sphere of Divine influence.[1]

What happens when Jesus rules our heart and takes the ascendancy over our thoughts, feelings, and will? *Revelation* rules our thoughts, *conscience* rules our will, and *communion* or *fellowship* with Christ rules our emotions.

Our heart must be open to both believe and receive. We must first *want* to receive. The second key to receiving is *belief.* Jesus tells us, *"If you can believe, all things are possible to him who believes"* (Mark 9:23). And, *"Whatever things you ask when you pray, believe that you receive them, and you will have them"* (Mark 11:24).

 **When Jesus rules, revelation rules our thoughts, conscience rules our will, and communion rules our emotions.**

"Bucket Man"

When Dennis was teaching me (Jen) how to drop down to my spirit, he used the analogy of dropping a bucket down a well. Focus is like a spiritual bucket inside. When we focus, we pay attention. He told me that when we focus on Jesus in our heart, we drop our bucket down to our spirit. However, when we focus on our own thoughts, we pull the bucket back up to our head.

> *Counsel in the heart of man is like water in a deep well, but a man of understanding draws it out* (Proverbs 20:5 AMPC).

Just as we can open our heart to the Lord or shut Him out, our choices determine the course of our life decision by decision. Therefore, we can clearly see that our heart has a door. The door into our heart is governed by our *will*, our faculty of choosing. When we open the door of our heart to God in prayer, we touch Him spirit-to-Spirit. When we *keep* the door open in everyday life, we begin to abide in Him as a lifestyle. We stay connected with the Lord.

To understand how we function spiritually, picture an old-fashioned well with a crank, bucket on a rope, and fresh, cool water deep down in the well. The crank is in your head and the water is deep within your heart—in your spirit being. The bucket is your awareness or focus. Close your eyes and open your heart in prayer. In your imagination, crank the bucket all the way down to your spirit, to the living waters in your heart. *"The water that I shall give* [you] *will become* [within you] *a fountain of water springing up into everlastin glife"* (John 4:14). Pay attention to your gut. (It's very subtle so don't expect fireworks or euphoria.) Maybe you'll feel something? Do you? Most people feel a mild sense of peace.

As soon as we drop down to our spirit and include the Lord, we should feel a gentle awareness that He is with us. We touch the peace of His presence. It is like a woman who is eight months pregnant. Throughout her busy day, she is continuously aware of the precious cargo within. When we have Jesus in our heart, we can learn to maintain a constant awareness of Him just like Brother Lawrence. Whenever I felt troubled, I realized that I was relying on myself rather than God. As soon as I transferred my trust to God, I could feel a gentle calmness and an assurance that God was with me.

We begin to a*bide,* or remain in God's presence when we stay connected to the Lord. As we learn to stay connected to Him in everyday life, we practice the presence of God. If you become distracted during the day and disconnect, don't become frustrated with yourself. Simply make the connection again. Drop down to your spirit. Remember, practice makes...permanent.

To teach the children in Sunday school this concept, I made a "bucket man" poster as a visual aid. Over bucket man's head, there's a crank with rope wrapped around it with a hole in the middle. A piece of string goes through the hole and is tied to a cardboard bucket to pull it up and down.

When the bucket goes down, we Velcro a piece of blue cardboard water to the bucket to represent living water; but when the bucket is drawn back up to bucket man's head, we remove the water. When the door of our heart opens to include God, our bucket goes down to the fountain of living water in our heart. The *"water that I shall give him will become in him a fountain of water springing up into everlasting life"* (John 4:14).

When we focus on our head, the door of our heart closes and our bucket goes up. A small child commented, "There's no living water in your head!" That was a very perceptive statement. When we focus on our own thoughts apart from God, our bucket goes up where no living water can influence our thoughts. The children love the bucket man illustration, but we occasionally borrow him to teach adults as well.

 **There's no living water in your head!**

If you ever sat quietly in church with an attitude of reverence toward God, whether or not you were aware of it, you most likely "dropped down" to your spirit. You may know intellectually that God is omnipresent, but when you focus on the fact that He is always with you, even at this very moment, your perception shifts based on this awareness. He is not only our Savior but our Immanuel, or *"God with us"* (see Matthew 1:23).

...I will never leave you nor forsake you (Hebrews 13:5).

God is our refuge and strength, a very present help in trouble (Psalm 46:1).

When we open our heart to include the Lord, the peace we feel is a gentle sense that Someone else is with us. It is much the same as driving a car with a passenger in the back seat. You may not be able to see them, but you know they are there. When Dennis was teaching me about peace and the presence of God, he reminded me to "include God" in the moment. For example, when I became anxious about something, he would tell me, "Open your heart to God and include Him."

I quickly learned that whenever I became troubled, I was actually cutting God out of the picture and relying on my own efforts. As soon as I acknowledged God again and welcomed His help, I felt calm. The more I practiced, the more consistent I became at including the Lord in everyday life.

As soon as I opened my heart to God, I could feel a gentle sense of tranquility and my perception of the world around me changed in a subtle but tangible way. It felt like an assurance that the Lord was with me. Peace is often so gentle it could also be described as "quiet stillness" or a feeling of relaxation. No matter how we describe it, the peace of God's presence is the opposite of anxiety.

The peace of God's presence is the opposite of anxiety.

Proverbs 3:5-6 tells us, *"Trust in the Lord with all your heart, and lean not on your own understanding; in all your ways acknowledge Him, and He shall direct your paths."* Notice that we are instructed to trust the Lord in our heart rather than relying upon our mental reasoning. The word "acknowledge" is *yâda* in Hebrew, meaning "to know" in a relational sense. It is often used for intimate union between husband and wife (see Genesis 4:1,17,25). As used here, yâda refers to divine intimate connection with the Lord. We make a heart connection with Christ in us when we drop our bucket down to our heart.

LOCATION OF THE WILL

The belly or gut is not only the seat of our spirit and emotions, but also of our *conscience* and *will,* the faculties of choice and decision making. The word "will," in some translations of the Old Testament, is translated *reins,* or literally our *kidneys.*

> *I the Lord search the heart, I try the reins* [kidneys]... (Jeremiah 17:10 KJV).

Door of the heart. The door of the heart is the *will*. It is in the belly. Scripture tells us that the door of the heart can either open or close, choose or refuse. Jesus says in Revelation 3:20, *"Behold, I stand at the door and knock. If anyone hears My voice and opens the door, I will come in to him...."*

Yielding. One of the most powerful lessons we can learn is how to *yield* our will. Unless this lesson is learned, believers will struggle in many areas of their Christian life. Yielding instantly connects us to Christ within. When we *don't* yield, we function by our own willpower! On the other hand, when we yield and connect with God, *God* works.

> *It is God who is at work in you,* **both to will and to work** *for His good pleasure* (Philippians 2:13 NASB).

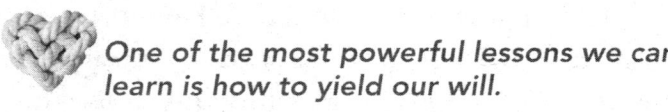 *One of the most powerful lessons we can learn is how to yield our will.*

TROUBLESHOOTING

Quite often, people who say they can't feel peace have an unrealistic expectation. Even an unbeliever knows if they're relaxed or stressed. As believers, however, relaxing allows *supernatural peace* to take the ascendancy and rule in our life in obedience to Scripture. Jesus has given us the gift of peace (see John 14:27). Peace should be the *starting place* for living the Christian life. The Scriptures command us to *"let the peace of God rule"* in our life (Colossians 3:15).

It is interesting to note that children never seem to have a problem feeling the peace of God's presence, although they sometimes use the word "good" instead of peace. However, adults often have difficulty when they have made a habitual practice of "compartmentalizing," or living out of their head rather than their heart. Our expectations and habitual way of life can make a lifestyle of peace harder than it should be. We must first *learn* to be still then *practice* peace in everyday life.

 *Most supernatural peace is too quiet for our flesh.*

Psalm 46:10 tells us, *"Be still and know that I am God."* "Be still" comes from the stem of the verb *rapha,* meaning "let go, surrender, or release." This verse contains two imperatives. We are to

first *be still* and then we can truly *know* the power of God in our life. We are not to intellectually understand the words but experience the reality of the kingdom of God at work in our heart.[2] In doing so, we are delivered from our fears and find supernatural peace: *"Surely I have calmed and quieted my soul, like a weaned child with his mother; like a weaned child is my soul within me"* (Psalm 131:2).

> But to what end are we to "be still," "let go," "surrender," and even to "die to ourselves"?... [W]e surrender *in order* to know that God is in control as *Ribbono Shel Olam*—the Master of the Universe. We "let go" in order to objectively know the saving power of God in our lives. We give up trusting in ourselves and our own designs in order to experience the glory of God's all-sufficiency.[3]
>
> *The Lord will fight for you, and you shall hold your peace and remain at rest* (Exodus 14:14 AMPC).

Although some individuals may instantly feel the presence of God strongly when they drop down to their spirit, over time the sense of His presence will increase for all. The absence of turmoil is a good starting point, but your awareness of supernatural peace will grow when you continue yielding to Christ within. The practice of *Christian meditation* is not merely thinking about God but surrendering our entire being to Him: *"... I meditate within my heart, and my spirit makes diligent search"* (Psalm 77:6). And: *"I will meditate on the glorious splendor of Your majesty, and on Your wondrous works"* (Psalm 145:5).

The Bible does speak positively about meditation. In the Psalms, David sings of meditating on the Law of God day and night. The biblical concept of meditation is not without reference to thought and content. To the contrary, it is about thinking that is directed by the Word of God—scripturally saturated thought.

> This is almost the exact opposite of Eastern meditation, which sets the emptying of the mind as its goal. The Eastern concept of emptying the mind is just not anything close to the biblical vision of filling the mind with the Word of God.... The biblical concept of meditation on the Word of God does involve an emptying, of course. We must empty our minds of ungodly and unbiblical thoughts, of desires for sin and resistance to the reign of God in our lives. But that emptying never involves an empty mind. Instead, it involves a mind in which unbiblical thoughts are replaced by the truth of Scripture—not a blank slate of meditation that revolves around the self.[4]

> *Blessed is the man who walks not in the counsel of the ungodly, nor stands in the path of sinners, nor sits in the seat of the scornful; but his delight is in the law of the Lord, and in His law he meditates day and night* (Psalm 1:1-2).

> ## PRACTICE
> ## YIELDING TO CHRIST WITHIN
>
> 1. Sit down in a quiet room and close your eyes. Place your hand on your belly. Relax and yield to Christ in you. Focus on your heart but notice that the atmosphere of the room also feels more peaceful. You become more aware of the Lord when you focus on Him.
>
> 2. Honor God by acknowledging the fact that He is with you. The Lord is not only omnipresent but you are also God indwelt. When you invite Him into your heart, He never leaves you.
>
> 3. Spend a few minutes waiting in the presence of God. Often, as we become more relaxed, our awareness of peace increases.
>
> 4. We should never attempt to make our mind go blank, but simply become aware that the Lord is with us by paying attention to Him. Focus is the opposite of "blank." We don't "empty our mind." We fill our mind and heart with God. [5]

Endnotes

1. William E. Vine, *Vine's Expository Dictionary of Old and New Testament Words*, Vol. 2 (Old Tappan, NJ: Fleming H. Revell Company, 1981), 206-207.
2. John J. Parsons, "Surrender: God's Irrepressible Care of the World," Hebrew for Christians; https://www.hebrew4christians.com/Meditations/Be_Still/be_still.html.
3. Ibid.
4. Albert Mohler, "The Empty Promise of [Eastern] Meditation;" https://albertmohler.com/2008/11/20/the-empty-promise-of-meditation/.

5. The Christian approach to prayer and seeking God is an active pursuit with the intention of quieting the soul (the carnal mind, will, and emotions) while focusing intently on Jesus. *"Let us go right into the presence of God with sincere hearts fully trusting him..."* (Hebrews 10:22 NLT). Thoughts, emotions, and perceptions are brought under the control of the Holy Spirit and yielded to the Lord. The goal is drawing closer to God. *"If a son asks for bread from any father among you, will he give him a stone? Or if he asks for a fish, will he give him a serpent instead of a fish? Or if he asks for an egg, will he offer him a scorpion? If you then, being evil, know how to give good gifts to your children, how much more will your heavenly Father give the Holy Spirit to those who ask Him!"* (Luke 11:11-13).

Chapter 7

DEALING WITH EMOTIONS

As mentioned previously, our emotions were created to be channels of the love of God. They were intended to be transmitters of the fruit of the Spirit (see Galatians 5:22-23). However, as soon as sin entered the world, Adam and Eve were taken hostage by the enemy and felt toxic emotions for the first time. Adam began to feel unpleasant emotions like fear, anger, guilt, and shame. Eve no longer enjoyed the tranquil paradise she had once known because her once peaceful heart became polluted with negative emotions. They suddenly felt the need to run from God when He came around to talk with them and made some bad choices. The enemy had hijacked their emotional pipelines!

 **Our emotions were created to be channels of the love of God.**

At the time of salvation, God rescued us from the enemy's kingdom. He *"delivered us from the power of darkness and conveyed us into the kingdom of the Son of His love"* (Colossians 1:13). We instantly received forgiveness and experienced peace with God. Kingdom emotions were restored to us and are tangible evidence that the kingdom of God is at hand: *"The kingdom of God is... righteousness and peace and joy in the Holy Spirit"* (Romans 14:17). And: *"the kingdom of God is within you"* (Luke 17:21).

Toxic emotions don't come from God's kingdom. They come from the wrong kingdom. We don't lose our salvation when we feel a negative emotion, but we take a temporary detour into enemy territory. The same answer that gave us peace with God in the first place—forgiveness—will keep us in peace when we live a forgiveness lifestyle. When we forgive, our emotions are instantly restored to the supernatural peace of God. As you received Christ...so walk (see Colossians 2:6). Peace is the evidence that nothing is separating us from the presence of God.

Emotions are friends that let us know what kingdom is in operation at any given time—the kingdom of God or the kingdom of the enemy.

 *When we forgive, we are instantly restored to the supernatural peace of God.*

Earth is our battleground (see 1 Peter 5:8; Ephesians 6:11). Christians are the property of God. However, negative emotions always give the enemy permission to attack us. The only way evil spirits can torment us is for us to give them permission. As long as demons have legal ground in us, they can harass us. When we remove negative emotions, we take back the ground. The enemy can't touch the fruit of the Spirit.

Like a flitting sparrow, like a flying swallow, so a curse without cause shall not alight (Proverbs 26:2).

 **The enemy can't touch the fruit of the Spirit.**

BITTER ROOTS

A bitter root is a personality structure that forms when a toxic emotion is planted in the heart. It takes root and grows up like a weed and produces poisonous fruit. Over time, sinful judgments form a root system that takes on a life of its own and operates automatically, coloring our perceptions, driving behavior, and causing cycles of trouble. As long as a bitter root remains, it continues to grow and inject poison into our life.

> *Pursue peace with all men, and the sanctification without which no one will see the Lord. See to it that no one comes short of the grace of God; that no **root of bitterness** springing up causes trouble, and by it many be defiled* (Hebrews 12:14-15 NASB).

> *...and judgment sprouts like poisonous weeds in the furrows of the field* (Hosea 10:4 NASB).

A root transmits either a flow of life or death, producing good or bad fruit. Your root system either draws nourishment or poison into your life and relationships. We can be rooted in God and life or rooted in bitterness, producing death. You can identify a root by its fruit. A root always produces fruit. Bad fruit comes from a bad root. Good fruit comes from a good root.

A tree is identified by its fruit. If a tree is good, its fruit will be good. If a tree is bad, its fruit will be bad (Matthew 12:33 NLT).

 **Toxic emotions are not sin; unforgiveness is sin.**

BITTER ROOTS AND UNFORGIVENESS

Bitter Roots Cause Trouble. Because many roots form in early childhood, we may forget about them as we grow older. Nevertheless, they still produce harvests of trouble in adulthood.

Bitter roots disrupt relationships. They distort how we see and understand God as well as how we see others and ourselves. *"Pursue peace* [forgiveness] *with all people"* (Hebrews 12:14) to be able to know and understand (see) the Lord. God ties forgiving people to knowing Him.

Bitter roots rob us of God's presence and power. Bitter roots cause believers to forfeit the grace of God that could have been theirs. See to it that no one comes short of the grace of God (see Hebrews 12:15). Grace is the personal presence of God enabling you to be who He called you to be, and do what He called you to do. Grace is not just favor, it is power to live the Christian life. When you don't forgive, bitter roots block the presence of God from working in your life.

Bitter roots cause us to reap bitter harvests. They result in continuing cycles of trouble and destruction. They also defile others, pushing them to sin against us. An individual who has been abused attracts abusers—until the root is removed. Any *"root* *of bitterness springing up"* has a life of its own, causing all sorts of trouble in unpleasant repetitive cycles (see Hebrews 12:15). Although it is not always obvious, one sure way to identify a bitter root is to pay attention to the bad things that happen again and again. We may even say, "Oh no! Here it goes again!" Or, "Why do I always get a difficult boss at every job?"

Bitter roots push others to sin against us. Individuals with a bitter root have something in them that causes others to react negatively toward them. Abused children often behave in ways that cause people to become irritated when they are with them. People who are wounded by rejection often have a "shell" around them that causes others to reject them or makes them difficult to talk to.

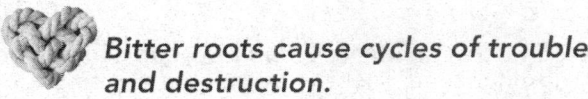
Bitter roots cause cycles of trouble and destruction.

Roots Can Drive Habits

Although roots are often hidden or forgotten, God will reveal the entry points in prayer when we ask. If we have a stubborn habit that has us in bondage, there is usually negative emotional power driving it and seducing spirits are often attached. (See Chapters 11 and 15.) Sin and toxic emotions give the enemy legal ground to harass us. Old-time Christians used to call these repetitive sinful behaviors *besetting sins.*

David offers us an excellent example of how to seek the Lord's help for cleansing our heart and removing barriers. David allowed the Lord to have full access to his heart. However, Psalm 19 illustrates David's process of approaching the Lord for healing and deliverance. He didn't try to figure himself out. David also admitted to God that he knew that the *unknown things lodged in his heart* could lead to very serious consequences.

> *Who can understand his errors? Cleanse me from* ***secret*** ***faults****. Keep back Your servant also from presumptuous sins; let them not have dominion over me. Then I shall be blameless, and I shall be innocent of great transgression* (Psalm 19:12-13).

JESUS THE FORGIVER

Jesus in us does the forgiving through us. Through grace we are saved, and by grace we live in the Spirit. *"I have been crucified with Christ; it is no longer I who live, but Christ lives in me"* (Galatians 2:20). Therefore, it is no longer I who love, but Christ who loves in me. It is no longer I who forgive, but Christ who forgives through me!

Christ the forgiver in us does all the work. And everything He does is easy for Him! All we have to do is yield and allow Him to work: *"It is God who works in you both to will and to do for His good pleasure"* (Philippians 2:13). What do *we* do then? We surrender our will to God's will and He does the work.

 Jesus in us does the forgiving through us.

THE PEACE OF GOD

Let's take a closer look at the *supernatural peace* Jesus has given to us as a gift: *"Peace I leave with you, My peace I give to you..."* (John 14:27). Jesus makes His peace available for *us* to enjoy! In English, the word "peace" is usually understood as tranquility or a lack of conflict. The peace of God, however, is so much more than that. When His peace rules our heart, we know Jesus is ruling in our life at that moment. He never withdraws His gift of peace so it is always available.

In *shalom,* Hebrew for "peace," we find completeness, wholeness, health, peace, welfare, safety, soundness, tranquility, prosperity, perfectness, fullness, rest, harmony, and the absence of agitation or discord. There is much more to biblical peace than tranquility or lack of conflict. Peace is the power that establishes the government of the Prince of Peace in our life. Peace is authority. Peace is power! When peace rules, Jesus rules.

WHEN PEACE RULES, JESUS RULES.

Peace, be still. From the place of peace, Jesus could sleep in the boat in the middle of a terrible storm, then stand and command the wind and waves, saying, *"Peace, be still!"* The same Prince of Peace who took authority over a storm on the Sea of Galilee also has authority over the storms of life.

When we walk in the peace that God gives, people and circumstances can't control us. Was Jesus ever frazzled or anxious? Of course not! He is the Prince of Peace. He has perfect peace, has authority to give us peace, and is the Commander of peace.

Romans 16:20 assures us, *"The God of peace will crush Satan under your feet shortly."* Peace is living in the presence of the Prince of Peace, for *"He Himself is our peace"* (Ephesians 2:14). When we are in peace, we are in the presence of God.

Forgiveness restores peace. If we happen to lose our peace temporarily, how do we return to peace? Forgiveness! Forgiveness always gets us right back into the atmosphere of the kingdom of God (see Colossians 1:13). When you got saved, did you have to wait to receive God's forgiveness? No, it happened instantly. Forgiveness is always available and forgiveness never fails.

We should let our emotions be our *friends.* They confirm the presence of peace and the absence of negative emotions. Once we know a toxic emotion is present, we can make a *supernatural exchange*. Any toxic emotion is a signal that the application of forgiveness is needed. When we present our negative emotions to God, He *transforms* them into Spirit-born emotions.

When we present our negative emotions to God, He transforms them into Spirit-born emotions.

How to Forgive

Important keys for prayer. Forgiveness is the answer for dealing with conflict and offenses in the moment as well as the baggage of the past. Christ is the Forgiver, so forgiveness works every time! It is instant, not a process, just like when you got saved. Deal with whatever God shows you, even if you think it is unimportant. There is no "big or little." If you think it is too traumatic to face, you only have to feel the pain momentarily to present it to Jesus for healing. It's all easy for Jesus! Finally, sequence is important, so always go in God's order. Pray through one thing at a time until you get peace.

Forgiveness brings roots to death. Jesus provided a solution through forgiveness. It brings bitter roots to death and replaces toxic emotions in our heart with supernatural peace.

Forgiveness is instant. When we got saved, we experienced instant forgiveness. Forgiveness is still instant in our Christian walk when we present our heart for Jesus to heal.

Who to Forgive

Forgive in Three Directions. Forgiveness goes in three directions—toward God, self, and others. Sometimes we must forgive in two or more directions. If in doubt, forgive. You can't love or forgive too much!

1. ***God.*** God didn't do anything wrong, but people get angry at Him anyway. Sometimes people feel hurt that God didn't do what they wanted Him to do, or become angry that God didn't *stop* something from happening. Forgiving God gets *your* heart right by releasing your judgments toward Him.

2. ***Self.*** If you are angry, disappointed with, or ashamed of yourself, you need to receive forgiveness for judging yourself so harshly. Frequently

people are much harder on themselves than other people!

3. ***Others.*** Release forgiveness to other people. It sets you free!

Removing Roots

We use what we call the Blue Card when praying forgiveness. It is not a method but the pattern we observed in Holy Spirit-led prayer sessions. Forgiveness removes the negative emotion revealing the presence of a root issue and replaces it with peace in supernatural transaction. Negative emotions are barriers to healing. If you are angry at God, start by forgiving Him. Most root healings require only the steps of first-feel-forgive. (We have the basic prayer steps printed on small index-sized cards we call the Blue Card.)

BLUE CARD

Pray. Get in an attitude of prayer. Close your eyes and pray, placing your hand on your belly.

First. First person or situation. What is the first person or situation that comes to mind—in an image or memory?

Feel the feeling. What is the emotion you feel in your gut?

Forgive. Yield to Christ the forgiver within and allow a river of forgiveness to flow from the belly until the emotion changes to peace.

Fact. After forgiving and getting peace, if there is a lie, renounce the lie out loud. Next, ask the Lord for the truth (scriptural fact) and receive it.

FILL. If there was an unmet emotional need: 1) forgive first; 2) release demands on people to give you what you needed; then 3) receive filling from Christ within.

Chapter 8

DISLODGING TROUBLESOME THOUGHTS

When we are born again and receive forgiveness, God instantly cleans up many aspects of our life. However, we don't know what He dealt with or what remains. Moreover, most of us spend years accumulating emotional baggage even after we are saved. It is a sad truth that most believers leave their church due to unresolved offenses. It is our responsibility to use what God has given us and cooperate with Him as we grow spiritually. We first know Jesus as Savior, but He wants us to surrender our thoughts, emotions, and will to His Lordship. When Jesus is Lord, we sense the peace of His presence. Our thoughts are conquered by taking them captive *"to the obedience of Christ"* (2 Corinthians 10:5). We vanquish negative emotions by applying forgiveness. Our will submits when we yield to Christ within.

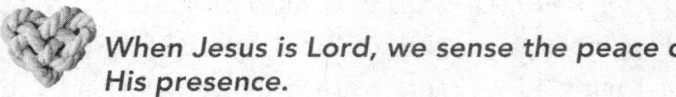

When Jesus is Lord, we sense the peace of His presence.

PUT THOUGHTS TO THE TEST

Both negative emotions and upsetting thoughts can trigger sinful behavior. A thought that upsets us has emotional power over us. Therefore, when we deal with thoughts, we must first deal with the *power* behind the thought—the toxic emotion.

Thoughts have two *tracks* through which they influence us. One track is the line of *communication* (hearing), and the other is the line of *authority*. We can't *silence* all the different "voices" but we can break their *power* in our life. The anointing breaks the line of authority but not the line of communication. Voices—the past, the world, the flesh, and the devil—do not stop speaking, but the anointing nullifies their *power* over us. Even though we may still hear a voice, when it has no authority, or power, we can ignore it.

We can't stop a thought from coming into our head, but we can defuse its power over our life.

Take responsibility for your thought life. Refuse to listen to wrong voices. Test voices according to the Word, the Spirit, and the fruit.

> *Beloved, do not believe every spirit, but **test** the spirits, whether they are of God...* (1 John 4:1).

 *Refuse to listen to the wrong voices.*

Test by the Word. Does the voice line up with God's Word? God will never violate His written Word—the Bible. Everything you hear from God will agree with the Bible. Obviously, the more Bible you know, the more you can recognize as scriptural or not scriptural. God will never encourage sin or violate a teaching in His Word. Does the thought line up with Scripture? Is the thought scriptural, or something God would say?

> *All Scripture is given by inspiration of God and is profitable for doctrine, for reproof, for correction, for instruction in righteousness* (2 Timothy 3:16).

Test by the Spirit. Does your spirit bear witness with God's Spirit? Any word from God has His nature attached! When you spend time with the Lord in prayer, you become familiar with His presence. His presence is pure, holy, and full of love. Even a corrective word from God has all the love of heaven behind it. When God speaks, His voice imparts life. When the enemy speaks, it is intrusive, negative, or seducing. The voice of the enemy releases poison, or death.

> *The [Holy] Spirit distinctly and expressly declares that in latter times some will turn away from the faith, giving attention to deluding and seducing spirits and doctrines that demons teach* (1 Timothy 4:1 AMPC).

Test by the Fruit. God's voice produces good fruit. Can you bear witness that the voice produces the fruit of the Spirit? If you listen to the voice, will it ultimately produce good or bad fruit?

> *You will fully recognize them by their fruits. …every healthy (sound) tree bears good fruit [worthy of admiration], but the sickly (decaying, worthless) tree bears bad (worthless) fruit. A good (healthy) tree cannot bear bad (worthless) fruit, nor can a bad (diseased) tree*

bear excellent fruit [worthy of admiration] (Matthew 7:16-18 AMPC).

TAKING THOUGHTS CAPTIVE

We must take responsibility for our thoughts to walk in true freedom. We should bring *"every thought into captivity to the obedience of Christ"* (2 Corinthians 10:5). How do we take thoughts captive and make them obedient to Christ in a practical way? We make distinctions.

1. Make a distinction: the new creation.

The real you is a new creation who loves God and loves His Word. The new creation always agrees with God. *"Therefore, if anyone is in Christ, he is a new creation; old things have passed away; behold, all things have become new"* (2 Corinthians 5:17). The new creation always agrees with God and His Word. If a thought doesn't sound like something God would say, don't accept it.

2. Make a distinction: inside or outside.

Differentiate between your flesh and demonic influence.

Check inside. When we feel something negative, we should first check inside. We feel our emotions *inside* us, in the gut. When we feel a negative emotion inside, we should deal with our emotions first through forgiveness until we feel peace.

Check outside. When we have peace inside but feel *external* oppression, the pressure is outside us. When we have peace inside, we have the spiritual authority and strength to resist anything negative in the atmosphere. If you accidently "own" a bad atmosphere outside of you, receive forgiveness and you will feel peace again.

 *Therefore submit to God. Resist the devil and he will flee from you.*

DISTRACTIONS AND MENTAL STRONGHOLDS

Categories of Thoughts

- **Simple distractions.** We give power to what we give attention to. When we lose our peace due to a mild distraction or fleeting worry, we should renounce it (silently or aloud). Release the thought into the hands of God until you feel peace again. When we *"take a thought captive,"* we give it to God.

- **Repetitive thoughts.** A repetitive thought with a corresponding negative emotion is a *mental stronghold*. If a lie comes in, it always comes in at the time of emotional wounding. (Most of the time, emotional wounds do *not* have a lie, or mental stronghold, attached to them.) When a lie *is* believed, it blocks the truth from being received. A lie becomes a repetitive thought that we hear repeatedly. A negative emotion is always attached to a lie.

Examples of Mental Strongholds

- "I'm unworthy." What does God say?
- "I can't do anything right." What does God say?
- "I never belong." What does God say?

- "I'm a failure." What does God say?
- "I have to have everyone's approval to be happy." What does God say?

Pulling Down Strongholds

Start with the emotion. To deal with a mental stronghold, always deal with the emotion first through forgiveness. When we have a negative emotion fortifying the stronghold, we don't have power to dislodge the lie. When we have peace, we have access to supernatural power over any lie. Always start with the emotion. When you have peace, you have spiritual authority.

Always start with the emotion

In approximately one out of 30 or 40 emotional woundings, a repetitive negative thought is connected, such as, "I don't belong," "I'm a failure," or "I'll always be alone." Assess the thought. Is it something God would say? Does it have the love of God attached to it? If not, don't receive it. Remember, if God didn't give it to you, you don't want it. If there *is* a repetitive thought, deal with the emotion first and get peace. Then, you have power to renounce the thought.

Dislodging Demonic Hitchhikers

Demons can't remain in an area ruled by God. We can't stab demons with a sword so they bleed and die. The enemy is *displaced* by the presence of God when He comes in. Light overcomes darkness. Unforgiveness gives the enemy legal ground, but repentance takes back that ground. Holiness purges out the unclean.

Dislodging Troublesome Thoughts

God's presence evicts evil and occupies the territory. When God cleanses an area in our life, His presence takes up residence. He occupies the territory. Demonic hitchhikers are evicted when God enters.

> *...When the enemy shall come in like a flood, the Spirit of the Lord will lift up a standard against him and put him to flight...* (Isaiah 59:19 AMPC).

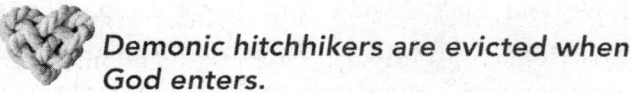
Demonic hitchhikers are evicted when God enters.

WEAPONS OF WARFARE

To mature spiritually, we must learn how to use our "God-tools," also known as *"the weapons of our warfare"* (2 Corinthians 10:4), and be diligent in applying them to transform our thoughts, emotions, and impulses (choices) *"into the structure of life shaped by Christ,"* and *"lives of obedience into maturity"* (2 Corinthians 10:6 MSG).

> *We use our powerful **God-tools** for smashing warped philosophies, tearing down barriers erected against the truth of God, fitting every loose thought and emotion and impulse into the structure of life shaped by Christ. Our tools are ready at hand for clearing the ground of every obstruction and building lives of obedience into maturity* (2 Corinthians 10:5-6 MSG).

At the time of salvation, we experience a great deal of transformation in our thought life, the choices we make, and our emotions. We gain clarity of thought as our hearts turn toward God. Many things that we could not understand before now become clear. Our preferences and actions begin to reflect our desire to love and serve God. We experience supernatural peace with God in our emotions. We are introduced to the fruit of the Spirit at conversion.

At the time of our initial salvation experience, we gain a great deal of freedom. However, many areas of our heart remain "un-evangelized" and don't yet submit to the Lordship of Jesus. The good news is that each time we cooperate with God in the ongoing process of sanctification, more and more of our heart is set apart for Him. In every area that comes under the authority of God, evil spirits lose their foothold in our life.

When you suspect that the enemy has some legal ground in your life or you feel like you are being attacked by the enemy, close your eyes in prayer and let the Lord show you the entry point for that attack. Pray the First-Feel-Forgive prayer steps until you feel peace. Let the peace of God rule!

> *As you have therefore received Christ, [even] Jesus the Lord, [so] walk (regulate your lives and conduct yourselves) in union with and conformity to Him* (Colossians 2:6 AMPC).

Chapter 9

Filling Emotional Needs

Emotional needs are *legitimate*. God gave us these legitimate emotional needs and also made it possible for us to receive what we require from our parents. A baby needs food and water, clothing, shelter, and love from parents—both physical and emotional sustenance. To have an emotionally healthy life, we require adequate foundations in the areas of trust, love, personal value, and purpose. Wounds suffered early in life can interfere with our ability to trust. A failure to trust produces fear. If you have difficulty trusting, however, God knows where that issue began in your life and is more than willing to heal and *fill* deficient areas.

Trust is the foundation of all relationships and our emotional health. It enables us to give and receive love, feel personal worth or value, and find a sense of purpose in life. If our foundation of trust is inadequate, our other foundations cannot form properly.

 **Trust is the foundation of all relationships and our emotional health.**

Ideally, parents should give their children good emotional foundations. Emotional wholeness is designed to be generational—a blessing passed from parents to children to grandchildren.

> *Fathers, do not irritate and provoke your children to anger [do not exasperate them to resentment], but rear them [tenderly] in the training and discipline and the counsel and admonition of the Lord* (Ephesians 6:4 AMPC).

When key elements are lacking in childhood, however, an individual may spend their entire life trying to meet emotional needs. Unfortunately, this pursuit is extremely damaging because people choose unhealthy ways of searching. Emotional neediness pushes other people away and robs us of the very happiness we are seeking. Most social and relational problems come from trying to meet our needs in the wrong way.

Most social and relational problems come from trying to meet our needs in the wrong way.

Emotional Black Holes

Legitimate emotional needs. We were created by God with legitimate emotional needs that need to be met. We need to have our needs satisfied to be properly prepared for life. Ideally, parents should give their children good emotional foundations. However, many fall short of the ideal. Wounds suffered early in life can interfere with the development of a healthy foundation. Traumas experienced later in life can also damage us emotionally.

SOME LEGITIMATE NEEDS		
Love and affection	Approval	Value
Attention	Belonging	Worth
Affirmation	Security	Purpose
Acceptance	Identity	Peace

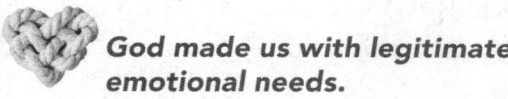

God made us with legitimate emotional needs.

Emotionally bankrupt parents have little emotional support to give to their children. They can't give something they never received. If their own emotional needs are unmet, parents can't meet the emotional needs of their children. No parent is perfect. However, a child's perception is often skewed. It is common for children to contribute to woundedness by their own misunderstandings. For example, a child who suffers from a chronic illness and must spend a lot of time in the hospital can feel alone and frightened despite the best efforts of parents to comfort them. Emotions are not logical.

Unmet needs in childhood result in *emotional black holes*. Individuals attempt to fill the inner cravings with substitutes that never satisfy. When individuals try to meet needs with counterfeits, they often develop soul ties with persons, places, or things (idolatry). Such soul ties have seducing spirits attached that cause an emotional "pull," so deliverance is part of healing. Substitutes are not necessarily bad in and of themselves. However, they become bad when we use them to meet our needs in an unrighteous way.

I (Dennis) grew up invisible to my father. He himself had been invisible to his own father. His mother had become pregnant out of wedlock so she and my grandfather had been forced to get married. He failed to ever acknowledge my father even though he accepted his two younger daughters.

My father worked hard and put himself through night school at Purdue University to get his engineering degree. When he finally earned his diploma, he came home quite pleased at what he had accomplished. However, when he told my grandfather, he failed to comment or pay any attention to my father at all. He looked right through my father as though he didn't even exist, and said, "Your sister made a Jell-O salad yesterday that was out of this world!"

Although my father loved and accepted my two younger sisters with no difficulty, I was another case. I would try to get his attention when he was watching television. For my effort, I just got, "Shhh. Shhh. Not now. I'm watching a show." However, even when he wasn't busy or otherwise occupied, he showed no interest in me. I felt unwanted and invisible. During my teenage years, I tried to fill the hole with girlfriends who gave me the attention I craved.

After I was saved, God healed me of rejection and filled the void with His divine attention, affection, and acceptance. The Lord said, "Dennis, I'm giving you My undivided attention!"

Filling Emotional Black Holes. Because people aren't perfect, God has made provision for healing and filling our needs. *"When* *my father and my mother forsake me, then the Lord will take care of me"* (Psalm 27:10). No matter what you've been through, God is able to heal you and provide what you needed.

HEALING CODEPENDENCY

In codependent relationships, one or both parties attempt to fulfill their emotional needs through their partner. They often go from one unhealthy relationship to another. Codependent individuals fear being abandoned or rejected and develop relational patterns of control and manipulation.

> Imperfect families often produce children who learn that to get their real needs met (safety, value, acceptance, etc.) they must give up important parts of themselves and conform to parental/societal expectations. The child learns the behaviors that will get these needs met. These behaviors may become patterned into codependency based personality roles.... When a codependent child takes on these roles there is an inevitable loss of the authentic self.[1]

It is common for a codependent individual to become a "rescuer" and get a sense of purpose through caretaking. They often alternate between fear of being abandoned and anger because they feel used.

> Codependency is...an emotional and behavioral condition that affects an individual's ability to have a healthy, mutually satisfying relationship. It is also known as "relationship addiction" because people with

codependency often form or maintain relationships that are one-sided, emotionally destructive and/or abusive.

Codependents have low self-esteem and look for anything outside of themselves to make them feel better. They find it hard to "be themselves." Some try to feel better through alcohol, drugs or nicotine—and become addicted. Others may develop compulsive behaviors like workaholism, gambling, or indiscriminate sexual activity....

As this reliance increases, the codependent develops a sense of reward and satisfaction from "being needed." When the caretaking becomes compulsive, the codependent feels...helpless in the relationship, but is unable to break away from the cycle of behavior that causes it. Codependents view themselves as victims and are attracted to that same weakness in love and friendship relationships.[2]

 *Codependents find it hard to "be themselves."*

Healing for codependency begins with honesty. The person must first admit there is a problem. Although you may have already identified some unmet emotional needs, in an attitude of prayer, ask the Lord to show you unmet emotional needs that are causing current relational problems for you and pray them through in His order one at a time.

Pray the prayer steps on the Blue Card, primarily First, Feel, Forgive, FILL. Deal with any lies (Fact), if any, and welcome the Lord to fill you when appropriate (see page 85).

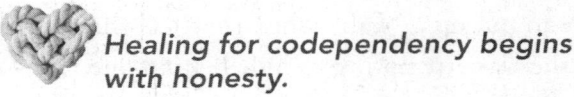
Healing for codependency begins with honesty.

HEALING

The counterdependent individual has unmet emotional needs complicated by walls of fear. An old "Garfield the cat" cartoon perfectly illustrates a common snare of the enemy—the two-headed dragon of fear. In the cartoon, Garfield bolts into a pet shop as a valiant freedom fighter and flings open the cages of the animals while shouting, "You're free! You're free!" However, the terrified cats and dogs cower in fear and refuse to escape from their cages. Garfield muses as he looks around, "Hmmm. Folks must not be heavily into freedom these days." He then slams all the cage doors shut again while shouting, "You're secure! You're secure!"

- Healing codependency requires filling emotional needs.
- Healing counterdependency requires removing walls of fear *then* filling emotional needs.

Unfortunately, we can create our own "cages of fear" when we believe our fear keeps us safe. Yet God clearly tells us, "Fear not!" We were ministering to Diana, a young woman who attended our church, and the first thing she pictured was hiding in her bedroom closet as a child while her parents had a knock-down, drag-out fight in the living room. However, she could feel no emotion in her gut, just a sense of numbness.

Hiding in fear had become her "strategy" to feel safe from the war going on between her parents. It is a common defense mechanism for people to put up a "wall" when they feel threatened, but in this case she was attempting to hide behind one fear—a demonic fear guard—to keep her safe from a bigger fear.

That won't keep us safe at all. It's like a two-headed dragon. One head doesn't keep us safe from the other because they are both our enemies. Diana first received forgiveness for using fear as a "shield," then she could feel the terror she had felt as a child. Now the core emotion was exposed. She released forgiveness to her parents and instantly felt the safety and comfort of God's presence shielding her from harm.

You, O Lord, are a shield for me... (Psalm 3:3).

In the case of a fear guard, deliverance precedes healing the toxic emotion and filling an emotional need. If you picture a frightening situation in prayer and can't feel a negative emotion, receive forgiveness for blocking the emotion first. You should be able to feel the emotion connected to the trauma instantly.

Removing Walls

Prayer should cover these areas:

- ***Forgive.*** Forgive whoever didn't give you what you needed. It will probably take multiple prayer sessions to deal with issues from your past.

- ***Release demands.*** Release any inner demand for that person to ever fill that need.
- ***Fill holes.*** By forgiving and releasing, you have created a capacity for the presence of God to fill the hole. Welcome Him to fill you in that area.
- ***Identify behaviors.*** In prayer, allow God to show you what you have been doing.
- ***Receive forgiveness and repent.*** Receive forgiveness for trusting in flesh instead of God.

Ask Him to guide you into a new way of living step by step.

Moving toward Freedom

Deal with your "baggage." Work through *The 60 Day Emotional Healing Challenge* found on our website, www.forgive123.com.

Be honest with God. Spend time in prayer and present your fears, hurts, and behaviors to God. Allow God to show you what is in your own heart. It is safe to be vulnerable with Him.

Be honest with others. Write down the behaviors you use to hide your true self (i.e., being silent, withdrawing, engaging in avoidant behaviors, etc.). Receive forgiveness for lack of transparency.

Be honest with yourself. Make a contract with yourself to begin working toward the goal of change: *I sincerely want to change and I make a commitment to be honest and take the steps necessary. I choose to face my fears and turn from manipulation in the attempt to get my needs met.*

Deal with denial. Ask God to show you where you are in denial. We may not see everything in ourselves, but God does. Some common forms of denial are:

- "Convenient forgetting" or deliberately overlooking the things you don't want to see
- Self-deception
- Lying
- Suppressing with willpower
- Justifying by making excuses or arguing
- Minimizing

Pray through the roots of self-rejection. In an attitude of prayer, ask the Lord to show you situations from the past where you judged yourself. You may need multiple prayer sessions.

Recognize passive behaviors and confront them. Honesty is the first step to change. Passive behaviors include:

- Feeling anxiety and restlessness when faced with a problem. Release the problem to God until you have peace then work on solving it.
- Trying to get someone else to take responsibility. Recognize avoidant behavior, receive forgiveness, and take appropriate action.
- Using manipulation. Receive forgiveness and ask for what you want instead.
- Rescuing. Receive forgiveness for pride and don't do something for someone that they should do for themselves.

Write it down then speak or act when faced with a problem. Doing nothing never solves anything.

Find a church home. If you don't already have a church home, ask the Lord to lead you to one and begin attending church.

Write down how you handle conflict. How could you handle things differently? You can talk to your partner about it. However, you can only change yourself. Unless your partner wants to take an active role, just work on you.

Develop assertiveness.

- If you think your partner will work with you as you change some behaviors, tell him or her that you want to communicate in a more direct way.
- Write down what you want to say.
- Ask for what you want. Communicate with your partner but avoid making your partner defensive. (Use "I want" or "I need" statements.)
- If your partner does become defensive, say what you want to say again but stay calm.
- Give your partner time to answer. Then come up with a solution to your problem together.
- Negotiate and compromise until you can agree.

Maintain proper boundaries.

Pray through childhood situations in which your boundaries were violated.

- Receive forgiveness for violating the boundaries of others.

Handle conflict productively.

Conflict can be frightening to someone who is codependent because it often triggers unpleasant memories. They find themselves torn between wanting to avoid conflict and wanting to meet their needs. Pray through the traumatic issues. You also might find it helpful to read a book, attend a seminar, or take an online course to learn how to handle conflict in a healthy and productive way.

STAYING STRONG

JASON'S STORY

One of the most important and difficult lessons I learned was that I couldn't be friends with someone with whom I had a soul tie. And especially not if sexual attraction was involved. I could be polite if I ran into them, but I couldn't be friendly or welcoming. Boundaries are crucial. If this is you, don't open your heart to them or give them any reason to hope. Sometimes it may be necessary to be blunt, saying, "I don't want to have a relationship with you anymore. I've moved on."

If I hadn't been surrounded by those who kept emphasizing this vital principle of maintaining distance to me, I'm not sure that I would have been successful in breaking free. A seducing spirit is like an umbilical cord looking for an attachment. All it needs is a little opening. It would be wise to make yourself accountable to someone who understands how soul ties operate. To stay free, stay strong!

> *Be prepared. You're up against far more than you can handle on your own. Take all the help you can get, every weapon God has issued, so that when it's*

> *all over...you'll still be on your feet* (Ephesians 6:13 MSG).

ENDNOTES

1. Patrick B. McGinnis, "Co-dependency: Abandonment of Self," January 9, 2001; http://www.dr-mcginnis.com/codependency.htm, accessed March 18, 2004.
2. "Co-Dependency," Mental Health America; http://www.mentalhealthamerica.net/co-dependency, accessed September 19, 2015.

 *Section Three*

Dealing with Habits

Chapter 10

LIFE, PURPOSE, AND TRAPS

by Dennis

Groundhog Day is a comedy hit movie released in 1993 that has become a reference point in the memory banks of frustrated and non-frustrated people everywhere. One group says, "That's like my life," and the other group says, "I'm glad my life is not like that!"

The movie is about a man named Phil, an arrogant and bored TV weatherman who has a yearly assignment to cover Groundhog Day in Punxsutawney, Pennsylvania. Phil grudgingly makes it through what he considers to be an idiotic ceremony. But when Phil awakens the morning of what should have been February 3, it is February 2 all over again. This happens the next day and the next and the next. Every single day. No matter what he does, Phil is stuck.

One night, as he sits at a bar in a melancholic state, he says to no one in particular, "What would you do if you were stuck in one place, and everything that you did was the same, and nothing mattered?" The equally sad man sitting next to him overhears and mutters, "That about sums it up for me."

 **What would you do if you were stuck?**

Phil was caught in a never-ending day. What about you? Most people want satisfying, healthy relationships. Most people want to be married to the love of their life. Most people want a home to live in, a job they like, and a car to drive. And everyone, in their heart of hearts, wants purpose in life. Destiny. A reason for being. But how can you ever get there when you seem to be trapped?

The bad news is that our own root issues trap us in the past. No matter how hard we try, our unresolved judgments and wounds can cause repetitive cycles of trouble that include unhealthy relationship patterns.

The good news is, things *can* change!

As believers, we have the most powerful help of all—God! We have the supernatural power of the Holy Spirit at work in our lives. However, just like Jason, we must actively participate in the process of moving toward freedom. The purpose of this book is to give you the same tools Jason used to get free.

 **The good news is that things can change!**

The Endurance of Unhealthy Attachments

Many years ago, a fellow pastor came to seek my help in dealing with something that greatly alarmed him. He was a happily married middle-aged man who had moved away from his hometown long ago. Much to his surprise, a former high school sweetheart moved to the city in which he now lived...10 years later. When they encountered one another, he was shocked to discover that long dormant feelings for her were rekindled. He came to me for prayer, broke the soul tie, and the arousal he had experienced toward her was completely gone. Unhealthy soul ties don't just disappear over time. They have to be broken in prayer.

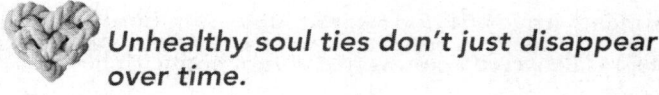
Unhealthy soul ties don't just disappear over time.

In another situation, a woman in the church I pastored came to me in desperation. She was a believer who was happily married with young children. A former boyfriend moved back to town. He wasn't a Christian and was addicted to drugs. She wept as she described the power of the emotional pull to be with him. Unfortunately, she refused to pray with me about it. Before long, I heard that she had left her husband and children to run off with the man. Toxic emotional attachments, particularly accompanied by demonic activity, are stronger than our willpower.

Deliverance from an Unhealthy Relationship

Susan, the daughter of a personal friend, came to us for help. She was in a toxic, on-again-off-again relationship with a young man. She broke up with him time and time again but they always got back together in spite of her better judgment. Finally, Susan made a prayer appointment to deal with it once and for all.

As Susan prayed, she saw the boy's face in her mind and felt the "pull" in her gut. I asked her to focus on the feeling and tell me if it felt clean or unclean. She identified it as both unclean and demonic. Susan was more than willing to break the soul tie through forgiveness. Then, as soon as she presented her emotions back to God, Susan instantly perceived that the tie was broken and exclaimed with joy, "I don't have to hate him but the pull is gone!" She was delivered and was free to move on with her life.

The pull is gone!

Breaking a Soul Tie with a Work Spouse[1]

A young husband and his wife had been fighting about his relationship with a woman at work so they asked if we would meet with them. She was jealous of what she called his "work wife" but he adamantly denied any wrongdoing. He said they were just friends. To put an end to the "he said, she said" argument, I told them we could settle the question once and for all by discernment.

I asked him to close his eyes, get in an attitude of prayer, think of his coworker, and feel what it felt like in his gut. As soon as he thought of her, he felt the attraction in his gut and a seducing spirit manifested powerfully. He opened his eyes abruptly saying,

"Wow! That's demonic!" You don't have to wonder if you have an unhealthy emotional attachment. It's discernable. We prayed with him as he received forgiveness and broke the soul tie.

Deliverance from Pornography

Pornography results in soul ties. It may not include a relationship with a real person but it does involve fantasy relationships. Late one afternoon a few years ago, a young man from my church called. Rob seemed both embarrassed and relieved when I answered the phone. He confessed that he had been looking at porn on the Internet for a while and now felt hooked by it.

 *Pornography creates fantasy relationships.*

I had recently spoken about the topic in a sermon, so Rob was emboldened to reach out for help. Most pastors don't teach about sex and sexual sin from the pulpit; however, I believe church leaders should freely discuss practical moral and cultural issues impacting believers and give them solutions.

As I prayed with Rob, we dealt with emotions and demonic hitchhikers[2] until he was free. A spirit of addiction lifted off in a release that was perceptible to both of us. Rob later described the working of this spirit in his life: "The pull was unnatural. I felt like it controlled me, making me do what I didn't want to do!" Rob agreed to touch base with me regularly for accountability.

Unfortunately, Rob's situation is all too common. Pornography has become one of the most destructive forces in society today. It is easy to access, and hard to resist. Even if the porn user manages to conceal his or her behavior, addiction is a difficult bullet to dodge. Fortunately for Rob, he sought help before his problem became severe.

Willpower is not as strong as spiritual forces. Spirit, good or bad, always wins. Methods and programs leading to abstinence can help weaken a bad habit, but true freedom comes only when evil spirits no longer have legal ground. *"Like a sparrow in its flitting, like a swallow in its flying, so a curse without cause does not alight"* (Proverbs 26:2 NASB).

 *Willpower is not as strong as spiritual forces.*

Free Indeed

In the following chapters you will discover what soul ties are, find out how they form, and learn vital keys for breaking unhealthy soul attachments and being delivered from the demonic pull! The devil doesn't play fair and sets traps for us that are intended to lead to our destruction. *"Be sober, be vigilant; because your adversary the devil walks about like a roaring lion, seeking whom he may devour"* (1 Peter 5:8). Don't let the enemy sabotage your destiny. God has a good plan for your life and wants you to be free!

If the Son makes you free, you shall be free indeed (John 8:36).

 God has a good plan for your life and wants you to be free!

ENDNOTES

1. The term *work spouse* refers to a person who has a job-related relationship with a coworker with whom a soul tie develops. The husband or wife of someone in such a relationship may feel a sense of growing emotional distance with their partner.
2. Toxic emotions, including lust and sin, attract evil. We refer to demons who attach to people because of emotional or other legal ground given to them as hitchhikers. When you take back the ground through repentance, forgiveness, and cleansing, demonic hitchhikers must leave. *"Submit to God. Resist the devil and he will flee from you"* (James 4:7).

Chapter 11

BREAKING BAD HABITS

We are creatures of habit. More of life than we might believe is the result of our habits—good and bad. Habits are behaviors that are repeated regularly and function automatically. Our habits shape the person we are and who we become. They either propel us forward in life or hold us back. Good habits are beneficial, but bad habits can sabotage our potential and destiny.

 **Bad habits can sabotage our potential and destiny.**

Habits help us through the day, eliminating the need to strategize about each tiny step involved in making a frothy latte, driving to work, and other complex routines. Bad habits, though, can have a viselike grip on both mind and behavior. Notoriously hard to break, they are devilishly easy to resume, as many reformed smokers discover.... Important neural activity patterns in a specific region of the brain change when habits are formed, change again when habits are broken, but quickly re-emerge when something rekindles an extinguished habit—routines that originally took great effort to learn.[1]

THE HABIT LOOP

Basal Ganglia and Related Structures of the Brain

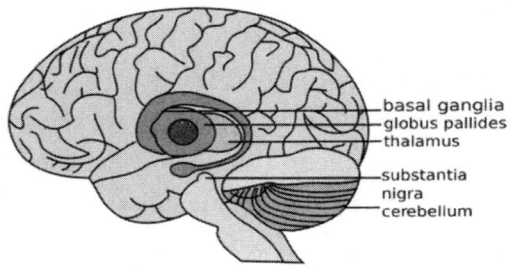

Ann Graybiel, pioneering neuroscientist at the Massachusetts Institute of Technology (MIT) has been at the forefront of research on habit formation for decades. The center of attention is a small bit of neural tissue called the basal ganglia. Until the 1990s the purpose of the basal ganglia in the brain was mostly unknown.

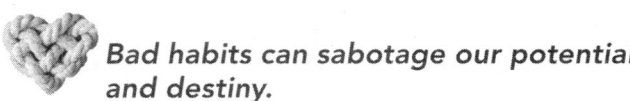

Bad habits can sabotage our potential and destiny.

We now know that this area deep within the brain plays a fundamental role in how we learn, process emotions, make decisions, and adopt habits. And that shift in thinking is due to the research done in Graybiel's lab.

Noticing that mice with injured basal ganglia had difficulty learning to navigate mazes, Graybiel asked, "Could the basal ganglia have something to do with habit formation?" To test the hypothesis, researchers used electrodes to record brain activity while the mice learned to find an edible reward, a piece of chocolate in this case, placed in a maze.[2]

Initially, the mice meandered through the maze scratching and sniffing at the walls. They could smell the reward so they were motivated to search for it. At first they had to really work at it, but running the maze became more and more automatic.

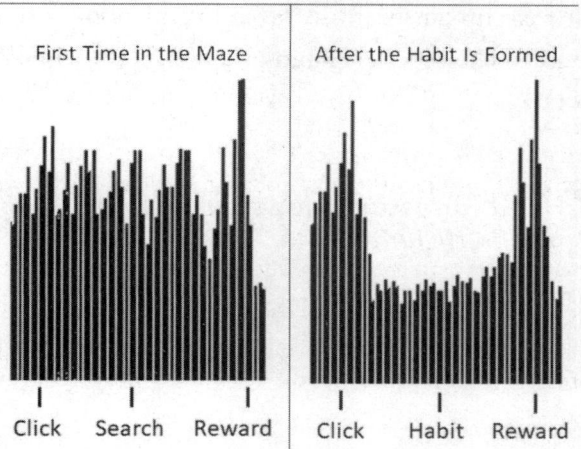

Habit Formation
Electrical Activity in the Cerebral Cortex

Soon it seemed as though they didn't even have to think about it anymore, and that is exactly what the brain probes showed. Activity in the cerebral cortex (the thinking part of the brain) went almost silent.

Activity even decreased dramatically in the areas related to memory. However, while the cerebral cortex ramped down, now the activity in the basal ganglia went into overdrive. Researchers concluded that the brain now stored a maze-running habit in the basal ganglia so the thinking brain no longer had to involve itself in the activity. It was put in the *habit box* of the brain.

The process that occurs when the brain converts a sequence of actions into an automatic routine is called *chunking* and is the root of habit formation.[3] A key piece of knowledge that proved to be very significant is that this habit was initiated by a clicking noise that acted as a cue to the basal ganglia that triggered the habit loop.[4] Trigger, routine, reward.

Scientists now know that it works pretty much the same way for humans. Habit formation allows our brain to work more efficiently. It frees up our brain so we can think about other things when we are in habit mode. Habitual actions free mental resources for other tasks.

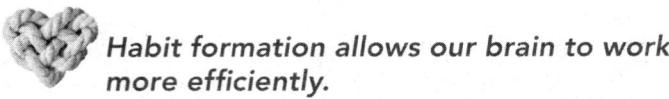
Habit formation allows our brain to work more efficiently.

THE HABIT LOOP

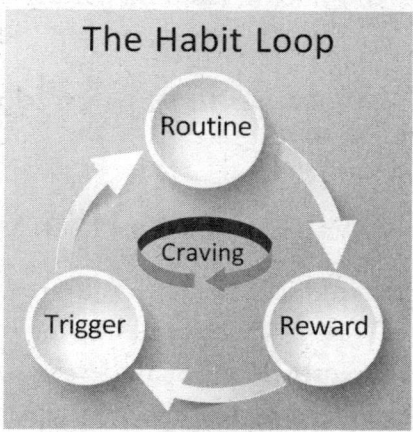

The habit loop has three parts: trigger, routine, reward (or cue, routine, reward).

Trigger. The trigger shifts our brain into automatic mode. It could be, for example, coming home from work, eating dinner, having family time, putting the kids to bed, and sitting down to watch TV afterward with a big bowl of ice cream. The trigger is putting the kids to bed.

Routine. The routine is getting a bowl of ice cream and turning on the TV.

Reward. The reward is eating the ice cream.

According to a 2009 study, there is no set time when it comes to breaking an undesirable habit. Some habits can be broken in less than twenty-one days, but the average time to lock in a new behavior is about two months.[5] It is much easier to break a habit when we substitute a replacement behavior.[6] Once we understand the process, we can create another habit to override the undesirable habit by breaking into the loop and altering the components.

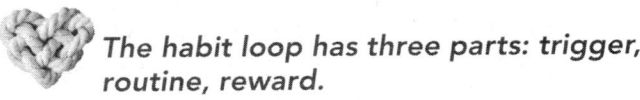 **The habit loop has three parts: trigger, routine, reward.**

CRAVING DRIVES HABITS

A habit is strengthened with repetition. What really gives it power is anticipating, or craving, the reward. Craving is the fuel of our habits. A pleasure center in our brain develops an anticipatory desire for the reward and we feel uncomfortable until we satisfy the craving.[7] Our brain anticipates the pleasure of eating ice cream but there's a gap between what we are experiencing and what we want, so we feel compelled to follow through. An unsatisfied craving creates tension that demands satisfaction.

 **Craving is the fuel of a habit.**

If we went to the refrigerator to get our ice cream and discovered someone else had eaten it all, we would react and get angry, hurt, or disappointed. Research has shown that monkeys in the laboratory can have temper tantrums or become depressed when they don't get their anticipated reward.[8]

The children of Israel had a temper tantrum with dire consequences due to a craving:

> *Now the mixed multitude who were among them yielded to intense craving; so the children of Israel also wept*

again and said: "Who will give us meat to eat?" ...Now a wind went out from the Lord, and it brought quail from the sea and left them fluttering near the camp.... And the people stayed up all that day, all night, and all the next day, and gathered the quail.... But while the meat was still between their teeth, before it was chewed, the wrath of the Lord was aroused against the people, and the Lord struck the people with a very great plague. So he called the name of that place Kibroth Hattaavah [graves of craving], because there they buried the people who had yielded to craving (Numbers 11:4,31-34).

ADDICTION

Craving is not only the fuel of habits, but is also the basis for addiction. Even though the line is blurry between habits and addictions, we do know that addictions are habits on steroids! They cause chemical imbalances to develop in the brain, alter the way the brain works, and produce physical withdrawal symptoms when the addictive substance is withheld. Addictions are marked by obsession that significantly interferes with important parts of life.

Addiction may be defined as repeated involvement with a substance or practice or to something that is psychologically or physically habit forming, such as narcotics, to such an extent that its cessation causes substantial harm because that involvement was, and may continue to be, pleasurable.

Toxic Relationships

In a very real sense, being stuck in a toxic relationship can be the result of a bad habit or even an addiction. Why is this? Most of us have a tendency to get into ruts. In an unhealthy relationship, many people feel that the option of leaving is more frightening than staying because they keep hoping things will change for the better, and maintaining the status quo requires less effort than moving on.

One way to break out of the snare is to think of it like just another bad habit and apply some practical as well as spiritual principles. All unhealthy relationships have a mixture of good and bad. It's the "good" that keeps us hooked. That shot of excitement when dopamine is released in the brain is like an intermittent pay-off for a gambler. It can add just enough excitement to override the toxic dynamics. Even a little bit of a reward keeps hope alive.

We have all witnessed it, and most of us have experienced it. Someone treats a person really well, and lovingly, and then... boom! Something extremely abusive happens. Healthy people do not tolerate that and they usually move on after it occurs a few times. Unhealthy people usually rationalize the behavior. Yes, he forgets my birthday, but he takes me on a great weekend get-away sometimes.

If someone does something nice for you, is he or she entitled to abuse you? The answer is no. Yet, more often than not, that is exactly what happens in many toxic, platonic, professional, familial, and romantic relationships. Many of us, with ailing self-esteems, allow people to abuse us because they have been nice to us. Why is that? There are two reasons.

From birth, the human brain's mission is to wire itself to best provide the highest quality of life possible. To achieve this end, the developing brain takes cues from our early environment to determine "how the world should be" and wires itself accordingly to survive in that world. This is why adults who grow up in unstable environments always expect the bottom to fall out when things are going well. When they were kids and things were going well, the bottom always fell out.

Likewise, people growing up with parents who were exceptionally loving sometimes and extremely abusive other times believe that is how the world is supposed to be. Thus, the mindset is: if you are nice to me, you are allowed to hurt me.[9]

The truth is that it's not okay to tolerate abuse and stay in bondage when Jesus paid such a tremendous price to set you free:

> *The Spirit of the Lord is upon Me, because He has anointed Me to preach the gospel to the poor; He has sent Me to heal the brokenhearted, to proclaim liberty to the captives and recovery of sight to the blind, to set at liberty those who are oppressed* (Luke 4:18).

Jesus paid such a tremendous price to set us free.

How to Change a Habit

Change is definitely possible when it comes to bad habits. If you have a soul tie, break it using the previously mentioned principles of prayer. Also, receive filling for unmet emotional needs. When

God breaks into the loop, rapid change can take place. If you have a habit you want to break, welcome the presence of God into the process.

Welcome the presence of God into the process.

If you want to change a habit, it would be helpful to identify the specific trigger-routine-reward components of the habit:

1. Determine the routine.
2. Find an alternate reward.
3. Pray through root issues.
4. Pinpoint the trigger.
5. Make a plan.

When God breaks into the loop, rapid change can take place.

BELIEVE YOU CAN CHANGE

The most important ingredient necessary to alter or break a habit is the belief that change is possible. In addition, having an accountability partner is very helpful when it comes to fortifying your resolve during the process.[10] What habit do you want to change and what is driving the habit? Is it a physical need or an emotional need? Is there a substitute reward that will satisfy the craving in a healthier or more positive way? If the craving is emotionally based, pray through the root issue behind the craving. After identifying the reward, identify the trigger, or cue, for the craving. Habit researchers have found that almost all habit triggers fall into one of five categories:

1. Location
2. Time
3. Emotional state
4. Other people
5. Immediately preceding action

After identifying the trigger and reward, you can start making a plan.

> "It seems ridiculously simple, but once you're aware of how your habit works, once you recognize the cues and rewards, you're halfway to changing it," [according to] Nathan Azrin, one of the developers of habit reversal training.... "It seems like it should be more complex. The truth is that the brain can be reprogrammed. You just have to be deliberate about it."[11]

An occasional slip doesn't seem to seriously impair the habit formation process. Gains soon resume after one lapse.[12] Depending on how deeply entrenched the bad habit is, overriding it with a new good habit could take a few weeks to a couple of months. However, you do have to be motivated and methodical or you won't follow through. Be patient, stick to your plan, and the habit will change.

 *Be patient, stick to your plan, and the habit will change.*

Endnotes

1. Cathryn M. Delude, "Researchers Explain Why Old Habits Die Hard," TechTalk (November 9, 2005); http://news.mit.edu//2005/techtalk50-8.pdf, accessed October 12, 2017.
2. F. Gregory Ashby, Benjamin Turner, and Jon Horvitz, "Perceptual Learning, Motor Learning and Automaticity: Cortical and Basal Ganglia Contributions to Habit Learning and Automaticity," *Trends in Cognitive Sciences*, Vol. 14, No. 5 (May 2010), 208-215.
3. Ann M. Graybiel, "Neurotransmitters and Neuromodulators in the Basal Ganglia," *Trends in Neurosciences*, 13 (1990), 244-254.
4. Charles Duhigg, *The Power of Habit: Why We Do What We Do in Life and Business* (New York: Random House Trade Paperbacks, 2014), 12-21.
5. Phillippa Lally, Cornelia Van Jaarsveld, Henry Potts, and Jane Wardle, "How Are Habits Formed? Modelling Habit Formation in the Real World," *European Journal of Social Psychology*, 40 (2010), 998-1009.
6. Ibid.
7. Duhigg, The Power of Habit, 19, 46-47.
8. Wolfram Schultz, Peter Dayan, and P. Read Montagu, "A Neural Substrate of Prediction and Reward," *Science*, 275 (1997), 1593-1599; Wolfram Schultz, "Predictive Reward Signal of Dopamine Neurons," *Journal of Neurophysiology*, 80 (1998), 1-27; Wolfram Schultz, Paul Apicella, and Tomas Ljungberg, "Responses of Monkey Dopamine Neurons to Reward and Conditioned Stimuli

during Successive Steps of Learning a Delayed Response Task," *The Journal of Neuroscience*, 13(3) (March 1993), 900-913.
9. Billi Gordon, "Hooked on Messy Loving: Why Toxic Relationships Are Addictive," *Psychology Today*, (February 4, 2014); https://www.psychologytoday.com/us/blog/obesely-speaking/201402/hooked-messy-loving, accessed October 19, 2018.
10. Arina Niktina, "The Role of an Accountability Partner in Goal Achievement," Goal Setting Guide (November 2, 2009); https://www.goal-setting-guide.com/the-role-of-an-accountability-partner-in-goal-achievement/, accessed October 14, 2017.
11. Duhigg, *The Power of Habit*, 46-47.
12. Benjamin Gardener, Phillippa Lally, and Jane Wardle, "Making Health Habitual: The Psychology of Habit-Formation and General Practice," *The British Journal of General Practice*, 62(605) (December 2012), 664-666.

Chapter 12

THE HABIT OF PRAYER

by Dennis

It's easier to change when you are in relationship with God than apart from Him. The best news for Christians is that we have God on our side. Knowing that in our head is one thing, but the fact that we have His help and can turn to Him in our heart is cause for rejoicing! The world muddles along with self-help techniques (which sometimes work) but we have the power of God Almighty at our disposal. *"God is our Refuge and Strength [mighty and impenetrable to temptation], a very present and well-proved help in trouble"* (Psalm 46:1 AMPC).

 **It's easier to change in relationship with God than apart from Him.**

A few years ago, a well-known minister took a short survey at her office of habits people wanted to make. Spending more time with God was right at the top of the list.[1] The most important habit believers can ever develop is that of prayer! Prayer is the foundation of Christian life. We say that Christianity is not a religion but a relationship. The only way we can develop intimacy with God is by spending time with Him. Our relationship with God is, or should be, the most important thing in our lives.

The best way to form a good habit is to make a decision to start, then, keep on doing it. Decide to make the Lord your top priority every day. All behavior starts with making a choice that leads to action. You might want to set your alarm and wake up a little earlier if necessary. When I get up in the morning, I get a cup of coffee and go to my chosen prayer space in the corner of the family room. My journal is kept beside my chair along with several translations of the Bible. (It's difficult to find time to pray later in the day because pastoral emergencies, texts, phone calls, and general church business guarantee regular interruptions throughout the day.)

 *Make the Lord your top priority.*

In a sense, a cup of coffee is my *trigger*. Prayer is my *routine*. The satisfaction of fellowship with God is my *reward*.

> According to a 2013 Pew Research Poll, over half of Americans pray every day. A 2012 poll found that over 75 percent of Americans believe that prayer is an important part of daily life.... Scientists have begun to consider the potential tangible (i.e. measurable) effects of prayer. This research suggests that prayer may be very beneficial.[2]

The benefits of prayer are scientifically-supported.[3]

1. Prayer improves self-control
2. Prayer makes us kinder
3. Prayer makes us more forgiving
4. Prayer increases trust
5. Prayer offsets negative health issues caused by stress

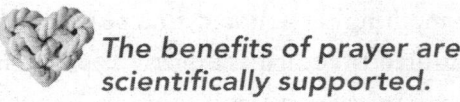

The benefits of prayer are scientifically supported.

My Prayer Story

The tan Oldsmobile Cutlass pulled up in front of the house and stopped. After a brief pause, the car horn honked then honked again more insistently. "Oh, no," I groaned within myself. A few more seconds passed. Once more, the sound of the horn exploded into the cold air interrupting my quiet reverie again. My now irritated car pool driver pressed the heel of his hand down hard on the horn in a prolonged blast!

It wasn't that I didn't want to go to work. It wasn't that I wasn't dressed and ready to go. It wasn't that I was busy doing something. The problem was that I was with Someone and I didn't want to leave. I was right beside the front door, kneeling in front of the sofa…lost in prayer. The presence of the Lord was so indescribably sweet that I simply couldn't get up. It was unbelievably difficult to tear myself away! With a twinge of guilt in my gut for keeping my ride waiting, I finally jumped to my feet, grabbed my coat, and ran out the door.

As a young Catholic at the time of salvation, I knew little about prayer and how other people prayed. However, as soon as I closed my eyes to pray, I *felt* the supernatural peace of God. Having always been somewhat hyperactive, peace of any kind was a new experience for me, much less the gift of supernatural peace Jesus gives to believers (see John 14:27).

I became acclimated to "touching" His peace and living in that atmosphere. Whenever something interrupted this peace (such as a negative emotion), I wanted to return as quickly as possible. Because peace is a gift given to believers by Jesus Himself, I understood that it was always available. All disruptions, therefore, were caused by me breaking my connection with Him.

My times of prayer did not consist of talking to God. Instead, I enjoyed His presence, touching His divine nature. Later, I read many books on prayer, but by that time, I was so addicted to just being *with* the Lord that I only had one petition and that was for more of Him. As a matter of fact, I discovered that in seeking God Himself alone, He always met my needs so I never needed to pray for "things." The Lord became my *"exceeding great reward"* (Genesis 15:1).

My guiding Scripture verse was Philippians 3:10 from the Amplified translation of the Bible, *"that I may know Him."* Years later I began to read Protestant books on prayer and was confused because there was so much talking involved. Convinced that my first approach, simply to enjoy being with the Lord, was so much more satisfying, that settled the question for me. Later, I called it *simple prayer*.

SIMPLE PRAYER

Simple Prayer is prayer focused on enjoying God. It is a life-giving relationship with the Lord. We spend time with Him and He imparts life to us. Paul cautions us to avoid being *"led astray from the **simplicity** and purity of devotion to Christ"* (see 2 Corinthians 11:3 NASB). Simple Prayer, therefore, is simply being in the presence of God.

Come into the presence of the Lord *expecting* to meet with Him spirit-to-Spirit. Present yourself to Him and yield your will. Drop down to your spirit and open the door to your heart to welcome His Spirit. Seek God for Himself alone, and make relationship with Him your top priority!

I suggest that you start by turning your heart to the Lord first rather than asking Him to meet your needs or praying for others. That can come later, but seek God, at first, for Himself alone. Communion with God allows intimacy to grow.

Meet with God spirit to Spirit.

THE PEACE OF GOD

God made us thinking, willing, and feeling beings. He also has thoughts, a will, and emotions. I learned the difference between the noisy chatter of my own thoughts, fleshly ways, and carnal emotions and God's *higher thoughts and ways* (see Isaiah 55:9).

The peace I felt in the presence of the Lord, I began to understand, was the *fruit of the Spirit!* We first feel His peace at the time of salvation, but it is meant to become our way of life. The fruit of the Spirit manifests as different expressions of the love of God.

> *But the fruit of the Spirit is love, joy, peace, patience, kindness, goodness, faithfulness, gentleness, self-control; against such things there is no law* (Galatians 5:22-23 NASB).

- One fruit: love.
- Joy is love rejoicing.
- Peace is love ruling.
- Patience is love enduring.
- Kindness is love caring.
- Goodness is love motivating.
- Faithfulness is love trusting.
- Gentleness is love esteeming *others as better* (see Philippians 2:3).
- Self-control is love restraining (subduing our desires for the benefit of others).

This way of prayer is both a *relationship* with God and a *discipline* that encourages growth of the relationship. Simple Prayer is not intended to replace other types of prayer. However, it does bring deeper meaning to all prayer, and leads us away from more active kinds of prayer into prayer in which we abide in the Lord and commune with Him.

> *Surely I have calmed and quieted my soul, like a weaned child with his mother; like a weaned child is my soul within me* (Psalm 131:2).

Two necessary ingredients of Simple Prayer are *silence* and *stillness*. If you have ever stilled your thoughts in your prayer time or church to quietly enjoy God's presence, you have already experienced Simple Prayer. The mind does not become blank—awareness of God increases.

 **The two necessary ingredients of Simple Prayer are silence and stillness.**

ELEMENTS OF PRAYER

Three elements of prayer include:

1. *Honor.* Honor God as a real person who is right there with you.
2. *Awareness* (touch, listen, feel, see). As you sense the presence of God, pay attention to the atmosphere and any spiritual impressions. Cultivate an awareness of His presence more than focusing on what you see and hear.
3. *Time.* Spend enough time to become still in God's presence.

The key to prayer, receiving from God, and developing our spiritual life is understanding *location*. We must know *where* to receive and yield. We must receive in our heart, not just our head. If we know something in our head but haven't received it in our heart, it is not yet real to us. Head and heart must cooperate in prayer.

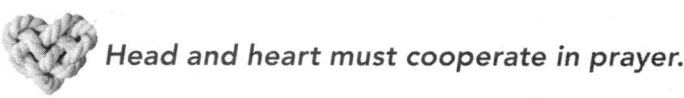 *Head and heart must cooperate in prayer.*

A HEAVENLY PATTERN

Those who truly love the Lord and make oneness with Him their main objective have God's pleasure as their chief desire. Our life on earth becomes significant in eternity when we are passionate about God's eternal purpose and co-labor with Him in fulfilling His eternal plan. God is searching for such sons and daughters. We have an inheritance in Christ, but the Father has an inheritance in us! Paul prays that we will understand *"the riches of the glory"* of the Father's *"inheritance in the saints"* (Ephesians 1:18).

The Lord told me that our relationship with Him only grows as we persevere in seeking Him. He revealed to me a clear pattern in the development of intimacy and spiritual maturity as well as the potential for both the increasing union and the tragedy of failure to continue at any point on the journey. The *"path of the just is like the shining sun, that shines ever brighter unto the perfect day"* (Proverbs 4:18).

The pattern the Lord revealed is this:

Touch leads to embrace. Touching the presence of God is wonderful, but that is only the beginning. Some believers wander from conference to conference hoping for a touch, but the touch that counts the most is the daily encounter in our prayer closet. Every time the Lord touches us, it leaves an imprint of the divine nature on our heart. When we persevere, the gentle touch becomes a holy embrace. In this stage, we must pursue a forgiveness lifestyle to keep the channel clear both vertically with God, as well horizontally with people. Unforgiveness is sin, and sin creates walls. Only sin can separate us: *"But your iniquities have separated you from your God; and your sins have hidden His face from you..."* (Isaiah 59:2).

Embrace gives satisfaction. Touch can be intermittent. Embrace, on the other hand, leads to a satisfaction that lingers. Embrace includes longing for more. We become strong in spirit with an increasing ability to quickly resist temptation. *"His left hand is under my head, and his right hand **embraces** me"* (Song of Solomon 2:6). Like Abraham, God Himself rather than the applause of people becomes the only reward we desire (see Genesis 15:1).

Satisfaction points to abounding love. Satisfaction leads to a bonding in spiritual union. It also includes a heart change toward other people. We become *"poor in spirit,"* or humble of heart, knowing that Christ is our life, and without Him filling our vessel we are nothing (Matthew 5:3). We see others in light of their great need for a new spirit. *"I pray, that your love may abound still more and more in knowledge and all* [true] *discernment"* (Philippians 1:9). When we have the eyes of Jesus, we have the heart of Jesus, and His heart overflows with love and compassion.

Abounding love reflects the Father's heart. We have moved from God outside, to God inside (the Replaced Life), to God Universal, the One who loved from the beginning. Our focus shifts from God as the One who takes care of me to the God whose love ever overflows on behalf of others.

The Father's heart brings His children to glory. We see the potential in people from God's perspective and long for them to know kinship and the way to "throne life." Because we now share the Father's heart, the focus of our heart turns outward to others.

Unlike believers who saw but turned away from this high calling, we long to become *teachers of others* (see Hebrews 5:12). God's eternal purpose becomes our passion and we willingly share in the fellowship of Christ's sufferings with joy (see Philippians 3:10).

To change our heart, or break a bad habit, we are not on our own. We have divine help! Although even unbelievers can learn how to alter habitual behavior, believers can rely on the power of God for wisdom, supernatural healing, and spiritual power.[4]

 **We have divine help!**

Breaking a bad habit *does* require commitment on our part. We have to want to break it enough to put some effort into it.

> Jesus did a hard thing by sacrificing His life for us, and He didn't ever say, "This is just too hard." He did it through prayer, constantly leaning on God, and having a strong commitment to doing the will of God. He, for the joy of obtaining the prize that was set before Him, endured the cross (Hebrews 12:2). As you begin your journey of breaking bad habits, keep the reward that you will receive in mind. We are motivated by reward, and God is certainly the Rewarder of those who are diligent. When you are weary…think of how wonderful it will be when a bad habit is broken and a good one has taken its place.[5]

KEYS TO FREEDOM

First, decide to get started. Second, maintain a positive attitude. Life is 90 percent attitude and ten percent circumstances: "I can do this with the help of God." Third, be committed. Don't let temporary setbacks discourage you. Next, have a regular prayer time in which you spend awhile soaking in the presence of God, not just talking to Him. Finally, welcome God into whatever happens during the day. Notice how your perception changes when you include the Lord. He fills what we present to Him. He is our Immanuel: *"God with us"* (Matthew 1:23).

ENDNOTES

1. Joyce Meyer, *Making Good Habits: Breaking Bad Habits* (New York: FaithWords, Hachette Book Group, Inc., 2013), 23.
2. Clay Routledge, "Five Scientifically Supported Benefits of Prayer," *Psychology Today* (June 23, 2014); https://www.psychologytoday.com/us/blog/more-mortal/201406/5-scientifically-supported-benefits-prayer, accessed October 2, 2018.
3. Ibid.
4. Meyer, *Making Good Habits*, 36.
5. Ibid., 37.

 *Section Four*

HEALING FOR SEXUAL ISSUES

Chapter 13

GOD'S WORD, WILL, AND WAY

God created man in His own image...
male and female He created them.
—GENESIS 1:27

Being joined in marriage is not the same as two people who choose to be roommates or tennis partners. Although marriage is also considered a legal contract in society today, it is primarily a spiritual covenant between one man and one woman. That's why it is called *Holy Matrimony*. It is a spiritual, emotional, and physical covenant defined and blessed by God Himself. *"Therefore a man shall leave his father and mother and be joined to his wife, and they shall become one flesh"* (Genesis 2:24).

 **Marriage is a spiritual covenant between one man and one woman.**

God instituted the covenant of marriage in Genesis as an enduring bond. A loving marriage between a man and a woman provides a stable home for raising children as well as mutual support and welfare of committed parents. The Lord gave sexual union as a gift for married couples to be enjoyed in a relationship made holy by that covenant.

 Sexual union is a gift for married couples.

Why did God do it that way? Why create one being and then take a part of that being and create a second, differentiated yet complementary being who is "bone of his bones and flesh of his flesh," a being who is sexually, emotionally, and in other ways different, yet of his own substance? Upon seeing her, Adam could have observed, "It's me...but not me." Well, if you think about it, it does sound like the kind of thing you might expect a Trinity to do.

The Trinity (Father, Son, Holy Spirit) is a family, and thus man in God's image must be made a family as well. Therefore, a man cannot completely realize the essence of his existence until he learns to exist with someone and for someone. Both relationship and communion are crucial to this process.[1]

Woman was created from the rib, or side, of the first Adam so he wouldn't be alone. According to the New Testament, the Church was created from the side of Christ, the last Adam, to become one with Him in fellowship and intimacy. *"One of the soldiers pierced His **side** with a **spear**, and immediately blood and water came out"* (John 19:34).

> For what reason is man to marry a wife? Because woman was originally a constituent part of man, she must return to become one with him again, so that the full expression and design of God's image in human beings can be revealed.... Sexuality, therefore, is a prefigurement of the intimate relationship that God desires to have with man. In fact, the marital union and covenant, in all its dimensions, is meant to gloriously reveal the very image of God in ways that we can only begin to understand.²

Just as Eve was to be joined to her source, Adam, and become one flesh with him, so we are to be united to our source, Jesus, and become one with Him. The *"glory which You gave Me I have given them, that they may be one just as We are one: I in them, and You in Me; that they may be made perfect in one..."* (John 17:22-23).

We were created in God's image as spirit beings.

Human beings are different from animals because we have spirits and are created in the image of God. As mentioned previously, our heavenly Father is a Spirit with heavenly DNA. *"God is Spirit"* and the *"Father of spirits"* (John 4:24; Hebrews 12:9). We were created in God's image as spirit beings. *"God said, "Let Us make man in Our image, according to our likeness..."* (Genesis 1:26). When we are born again, our capacity to touch God in the spiritual realm is restored.

Pierre Teilhard de Chardin writes, in *The Phenomenon of Man,* "We are not human beings having a spiritual experience; we are spiritual beings having a human experience."³

Human sexuality contains a force so powerful it can bring forth a *human life* into existence. Our children are born as spirit beings who can become children of God. That is why moral purity is so important. The Bible tells us what to avoid and what to do to keep us safe, not to spoil our fun, but because the penalty for sexual sin is so severe. Keeping God's moral commandments keeps us from being defiled by demons. Sexual sin is such a serious violation that evil spirits always attach when sexual sin is committed.

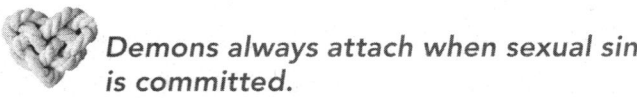

Demons always attach when sexual sin is committed.

MARRIAGE IS A SPIRITUAL COVENANT

Because marriage is a covenant instituted by God, only He can define its proper use. The Bible clearly says sex was made only for a man and woman in a covenant marriage sanctioned by God. Any other expression of human sexuality is sinful and an abuse of God's gift. It does not make something less sinful or the consequences less severe just because "everybody's doing it."

Sex was a special gift from God that was reserved exclusively for couples within the marriage covenant. The sexual act was designed by God to be enjoyed within marriage as demonstration of biblical oneness. Marriage was intended to be one complete package with unique responsibilities and blessings. Marriage was designed to bring joy and satisfaction, grow the human race, be a building block of society, and reproduce godly children.

ONE FLESH BOND

A man will *"leave his father and mother and be joined to his wife, and they shall become **one flesh**"* (Genesis 2:24). The term *one flesh* means that the spirits of husband and wife joined together. A spiritual bond has been created. Husband and wife become one—spirit, soul, and body. A spiritual bond is also created by a sinful sexual union but that union is ruled by evil spirits.

> *Do you not know that **your bodies are members of Christ? Shall I then take the members of Christ and make them members of a harlot?** Certainly not! Or do you not know that **he who is joined to a harlot is one body with her?** For "the two," He says, "shall **become one flesh**"* (1 Corinthians 6:15-16).

SEXUAL IMMORALITY

The world today is much like that of ancient Israel during the Book of Judges. It was a time of anarchy and *"everyone did what was right in his own eyes"* (Judges 17:6). The Word of God wasn't their standard; they made up their own rules. God doesn't change and His Word doesn't change. The Lord is our Judge, the Ruler of the universe, and His Word is absolute truth. *"The grass withers, the flower fades, but the word of our God stands forever"* (Isaiah 40:8).

God is still the same and His Word is still truth: *"Forever, O Lord, Your word is settled in heaven"* (Psalm 119:89). And: *"The word of the Lord endures forever"* (1 Peter 1:25).

With the coming of Jesus, the shadow and type of Old Covenant, Mosaic law passed away because the One who was the fulfillment of the Law had come. However, Jesus Himself assures us that the moral commandments of the Old Testament are still valid. Without moral law, the Ten Commandments would no longer apply to us. It would be acceptable to God for us to worship idols, murder, steal, lie, covet, and commit adultery. Jesus declares,

> *Do not think that I came to destroy the Law or the Prophets.* ***I did not come to destroy but to fulfill.*** *For assuredly,* ***I say to you, till heaven and earth pass away, one jot or one tittle will by no means pass from the law till all is fulfilled*** (Matthew 5:17-18).

 **The moral commandments of the Old Testament are still valid.**

Christ in Us

What does it mean that Christ came to *"fulfill the law"*? The law was given to reveal our inability to keep it in our fallen human condition. We can't live the Christian life. Only Christ is capable of living the Christian life. He first fulfilled the perfect law of God. Now He fulfills it through us. We are vessels, or containers. The purpose of a vessel is to contain something. In our case, to be filled with Someone: *Christ in us, the hope of glory* (Colossians.

1:27). Therefore, when Christ dwells in us, He lives in us to keep God's moral law. As we yield, He lives His life through us.

Moreover, instead of doing away with or relaxing the requirements of God, Jesus raised the Old Testament standard for morality to include holiness of heart under the New Covenant:

> *I say to you that **whoever looks at a woman to lust for her has already committed adultery with her in his heart*** (Matthew 5:28).

Jesus raised the standard to include holiness of heart.

In Adam, we inherited two problems—*sins* committed and a *wrong spirit* filling us. In Christ, God provides a two-fold redemption: the blood and the Cross. We receive forgiveness of our sins through His shed blood: *"In Him we have redemption through His blood, the forgiveness of sins..."* (Ephesians 1:7). Our second dilemma is the presence of a *wrong spirit* in us, or a sin nature, governed by the law of sin and death (see Romans 8:2). Therefore, we need a *new Spirit!* That is also accomplished by the work of the Cross.

Jesus took all humanity with Him when He died on the Cross. We died when He died. Because our spirit leaves our body when we die, the sin spirit, or nature, left when we died with Christ. *"The body without the spirit is dead"* (James 2:26). Because we died, we died to the infilling of the wrong spirit so we could be filled with another Spirit—the Spirit of God. When Christ was raised from the dead, we were raised together with Him with a *new spirit*. We received *"newness of life"* (Romans 6:4). The indwelling sin spirit was *replaced* by the Spirit of Christ! When Christ was raised by the power of the Father, we were raised together with Him with a *new spirit*.

Our life replaced by Christ's life gives us:

- The Spirit of Life instead of a spirit of death
- The Spirit of Truth instead of a spirit of error
- The True Vine (source of living) instead of a false vine
- The Spirit of Holiness instead of a spirit of sin

God doesn't make *us* good, because there is no goodness in us. God doesn't make *us* loving, because human love falls short of God's love. God doesn't make *us* holy, because only He is holy. For every need, God gives us Christ: *"By His doing you are in Christ Jesus, who became to us wisdom from God, and righteousness and sanctification* [holiness], *and redemption"* (1 Corinthians 1:30 NASB). And: *"...it is no longer I who live, but Christ lives in me..."* (Galatians 2:20).

 **For every need, God gives us Christ.**

It was impossible for us to live the Christian life all along. "We are forced to admit that we cannot manifest godliness apart from God, or righteousness apart from the Righteous One, Jesus Christ. The Christian life is Christ's life lived out in us, as us, and through us, while we as dependent creatures derive [everything]

from Him."4 Through a replaced life, we no longer manifest a wrong spirit, but Christ's Spirit.

The Christian life is Christ's life lived out in us, as us, and through us.

SPIRIT-SOUL-BODY CONNECTION

Our spirit, soul, and body are connected as a single entity. Whatever affects the body impacts the soul and spirit. Everything that happens to one part impacts the others. Whatever happens to our body touches our soul and spirit. We are fashioned as an indivisible unit!

> *Now may the God of peace Himself sanctify you completely; and may your whole* **spirit, soul, and body** *be preserved blameless at the coming of our Lord Jesus Christ* (1 Thessalonians 5:23).

We are fashioned as an indivisible unit—spirit, soul, and body!

THE WORD, WILL, AND WAY OF GOD

God is Absolute Authority. Guidance in right living is established by 1) God's Word; 2) God's will; and 3) God's way. God's Word is truth. God's will is oneness. God's way is love.

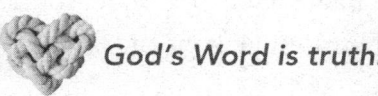
God's Word is truth.

In the following areas the Word of God is clear and quite specific sinful behavior: fornication, adultery, incest, bestiality, homosexuality, and so forth (Leviticus 18:20-23; 1 Corinthians 5:1; 6:13-20; Galatians 5:19; Jude 1:7). These are just a few of the Scriptures that address the broad spectrum of what is covered in the Bible concerning sexual activity; but there are some other areas that are not covered specifically such as dating, oral sex, masturbation, and so forth. To properly clarify the topics that are not clearly defined in the Word of God, we must also consider God's will and God's way.

 God's will is oneness.

The ultimate intent of God in the sacrifice of Christ on the cross was the restoration of the unity, oneness, between God and man and between people (Ephesians 2:1-19). When Adam sinned in the Garden of Eden, the unity between God and His creation was fractured. Salvation is individual, of course, but God's will is corporate for unity. The Bible warns against sexual sin 1) so we will not forfeit the blessings He has for us, and 2) we won't be defiled by evil spirits. There are some sins that don't automatically result in demonic attachment, but sexual sin instantly opens the door for seducing spirits.

 God's way is love.

God's way is *always* love. God *is* love. God loves so much that He gave His only Son for sinful humankind. Jesus laid down His own life to redeem us. Jesus loved so much that He forgave even while an angry mob was nailing Him to the cross (see Luke 23:34).

> But God demonstrates His own love toward us, in that while we were still sinners, Christ died for us (Romans 5:8).

> This is My commandment, that you love one another as I have loved you (John 15:12).

> By this we know love, because He laid down His life for us. And we also ought to lay down our lives for the brethren (1 John 3:16).

> Greater love has no one than this, than to lay down one's life for his friends (John 15:13).

SAFETY OR VIOLATION

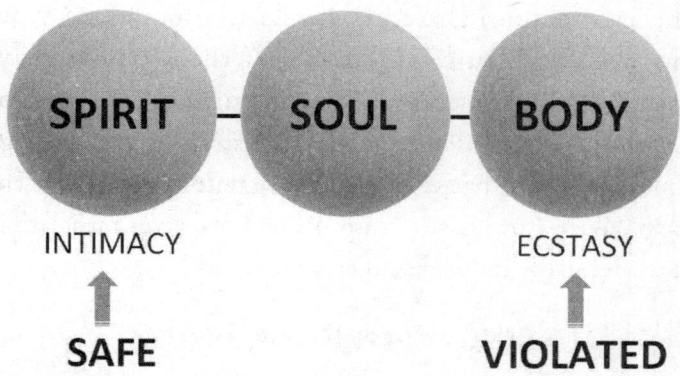

Within the marriage covenant and loving relationship there should be *safety*. This leaves no room for either partner to use manipulation, pressure, or selfishness in the marital union. Does your partner feel safe or feel violated in your marriage bed? As a husband, do you pressure your mate to do something that violates her conscience? As a wife, do you use sex to manipulate and control?

> *Husbands, love your wives, just as Christ also loved the church and gave Himself for her* (Ephesians 5:25).
>
> *Nevertheless, let each one of you in particular so love his own wife as himself, and let the wife see that she respects her husband* (Ephesians 5:33).

When sex is misused for selfish physical gratification, it always produces a sense of violation because it was created for oneness, trust, and understanding. Instinctively, a woman feels used and violated when her partner uses her for a cheap thrill, or physical ecstasy, which is selfish gratification. But men also feel used when a woman uses sex for leverage or manipulation.

Both men and women have an inner longing for intimacy with a partner. Sex is truly satisfying only within the safety of a loving relationship. Casual sex violates a woman's fundamental makeup that longs for home and security. Demonstrating love through giving pleasure to the partner is selfless in nature. Love wants to increase oneness. Love desires to protect. Love gives rather than takes. Lust is selfish and seeks only to please self.

Dealing with Root Issues

God causes root issues to manifest so we can cleanse our heart. Don't blame it all on the devil! Marriage will reveal our weak points so we can deal with them and grow closer. God's purpose was oneness, but couples grow closer as they allow the Lord to deal with their issues and live a lifestyle of forgiveness in marriage.

Society. Society bombards us with unhealthy representations of sex. The culture in which we live is filled with casual sex and sexual imagery. Movies, magazines, and books encourage sexual activity. The Internet has made it easy to get addicted to pornography in the privacy of one's own home. At one time, people had to go out of their way to have access to such materials.

 *God causes root issues to manifest so we can cleanse our heart.*

Childhood experimentation and abuse. The occurrence of childhood experimentation, emotional and physical soul ties, abuse and molestation, the viewing of suggestive movies and pornography, and sexual contact is so widespread that hardly anyone reaches adulthood completely unscathed. A child who has been sexually abused has a confused conscience. When they grow up, they won't be able to tell the difference between love and lust.

A child who has been sexually molested will be targeted by other molesters. Childhood experimentation can establish unhealthy patterns for adulthood fetishes and perversions. Deviant patterns are hardwired into the brain through neural pathways. Fortunately, the brain can be remapped through prayer and healthy relationships.

Discerning seducing spirits. Once there has been sexual compromise, seducing spirits are involved. Seducing spirits attract one another, and draw couples together through lust. When it is done right, marriages should be made in heaven. God wants to join the right men and women together in marriage. Unfortunately, the devil uses lust to create marriages made in hell.

Believers need to understand the benefits of chastity, the consequences of sexual compromise, and have the tools to get free. In addition, believers must exercise spiritual discernment to detect the presence of seducing spirits. A seducing spirit attaches to lust. It has drawing power, or pull, like a spiritual umbilical cord looking for a place to attach. Seducing spirits are given permission to infest a person's life when sexual sin is committed.

> **When a couple gets married, seducing spirits from previous relationships bring division.**

Seducing spirits and soul ties. Demons do not mold to *all* fleshly manifestations, inner wounds, or sin—but sexual sins automatically give legal ground to demons. Seducing spirits are *given permission* when sexual sin is committed. They only leave when forgiveness and cleansing are applied. It doesn't matter whether or not there has been actual physical involvement, seducing spirits can also link to emotional attachments when there has been no physical contact.

> **Sexual sins automatically give legal ground to demons.**

Sexual soul ties. A sexual soul tie is an impure emotional connection with a seducing spirit attached. A soul tie does not disappear over time and can resurface many years later. A person can see a former girlfriend or boyfriend after a span of decades, and there will be instantaneous attraction. Even when someone has been the victim of rape or molestation, a soul tie is formed. The devil doesn't care if we are the victim or perpetrator, the innocent or guilty party.

Soul ties with parents. Parents can develop ungodly soul ties with their children and vice versa. Parental inversion or substitute mate relationships may occur.[5] I (Dennis) once had an appointment with a man whose complaint was that his mother constantly interfered in his marriage. Both husband and wife were extremely frustrated. When he and I prayed together, we dealt with root issues concerning his mother then broke the soul tie. He could sense that something unclean was severed at that very moment. Immediately after the prayer session, his mother called to confront him saying, "Why did you cut me off? I can feel it!" Although she was angry at first, she eventually agreed to abide by his boundaries. The wife was very grateful to "have her husband back."

Spiritual adultery. If a married person develops an emotional attraction with a person other than a spouse, he or she is entering into spiritual adultery. As soon as emotional bonding or physical desire (passion) begins to be aroused, human spirits begin to form an unholy one-flesh covenant bond, and seducing spirits mold around it. This phenomenon is so prevalent in the workplace that the expression "work spouse" has become common. If spiritual adultery is not dealt with, it will almost certainly escalate to physical adultery. Believers must also continue to be vigilant after breaking a soul tie because the other party will often attempt to reestablish the connection.

> *You know the next commandment pretty well, too: "Don't go to bed with another's spouse." But don't think*

you've preserved your virtue simply by staying out of bed. Your heart can be corrupted by lust even quicker than your body. Those leering looks you think nobody notices—they also corrupt (Matthew 5:27-28 MSG).

 *If spiritual adultery is not dealt with, it will almost certainly escalate to physical adultery.*

Communication. The best way for safety in marriages is open communication between partners. If one feels any attraction to someone other than their spouse, share that information immediately. Check to see if there is a soul tie and receive forgiveness. If your spouse is uncomfortable with your relationship with another person, that is a red flag that something is wrong. Listen to your spouse. Do not share your life on any emotional level with anyone other than your partner or a same-sex friend. Do not keep secrets from your spouse. At work or in a business setting, keep it strictly business.

Healing. In prayer, think of the person. Feel the feeling. If there is even the slightest arousal or excitement, receive forgiveness, forgive the other person involved. Break the soul tie and give your emotions back to God.

Caution. Of course, this applies in a healthy, honest relationship. If a partner is overly suspicious, jealous, and possessive, you have another problem to deal with.

Soul tie with spouse. Occasionally, after a divorce or the death of a spouse, a familiar spirit may harass through sexual or tormenting dreams if a soul tie is still intact. When the soul tie is severed and the area is cleansed, the dreams cease.

Spirit Is Stronger than Willpower

Many Christians, including leaders in the body of Christ, have open doors in their lives, but are able to resist temptation for many years before falling into sin. However, spiritual law is stronger than willpower. The enemy has the capacity to be very patient and wait for an opportune time. He knows how to bring the perfect amount of pressure to push a believer into sin if there is a chink in the armor.

Start with the Emotions

To deal effectively with sexual issues, you must *start* with the emotion. Why? Sex is always emotional—it involves either love or lust. There is no such thing as non-emotional sexual acts. Love cares more about the other person than oneself. Love gives. Love protects. Lust is selfish and self-focused. Lust is a magnet for demonic hitchhikers. To bring cleansing and deliverance, the emotions must be impacted at points of entry. When the emotions are dealt with properly, the enemy no longer has legal ground.

To deal effectively with sexual issues, you must start with the emotions.

Entry points

Failure to deal with entry points from the past leaves you vulnerable to ongoing demonic pressure. Many believers try to resist through willpower, but willpower is *flesh*. Spirit, good or evil, is stronger than flesh, and the enemy knows how to set traps that eventually cause believers to fall into sin.

Surely He shall deliver you from the snare of the fowler... (Psalm 91:3).

 *Spirit, good or evil, is stronger than flesh.*

Closing Open Doors—The Wrong Way

Suppression by willpower. Willpower is flesh. It can only suppress appetites and desires so long before weakening and giving in. Spirit, good or evil, is stronger than willpower.

Maintaining with willpower. Many individuals have a soul tie or other open door from the past. The enemy can apply the ongoing pressure of temptation, and he knows how to set traps for those who are vulnerable. Unfortunately, most believers don't know how to truly be set free, so they try to resist with willpower. When there is an open door, willpower can weaken over time, or the "right" circumstances can push you to the point where willpower is not strong enough to resist.

Self-protection by willpower walls. Self-protection in the flesh is a form of fear. When you try to "protect" yourself from relationships or members of the opposite sex by using willpower, you have flesh walls up. You can't discern properly through walls and you block the release of anointing through you on behalf of others.

Shutting down emotionally. When you shut down emotionally, you are withholding your emotions from God and others. You *close your heart*. Your emotions belong to God. You are not your own. You were purchased by God, and you don't have a right to withhold your emotions from Him. He created your emotions to be *open* conduits of the fruit of the Spirit.

> *Do you not know that your body is the temple of the Holy Spirit who is in you, whom you have from God, and you are not your own? For you were bought at a price; therefore glorify God in your body and in your spirit, which are God's* (1 Corinthians 6:19-20).

HEALING SEXUAL ISSUES—THE RIGHT WAY

The right way to deal with sexual sin is let God bring to mind individual situations, feel the emotion, and present it to God for cleansing and deliverance. God has already given all believers the God-tools they need, so you can learn to apply them in your own life.

ENDNOTES

1. David Kyle Foster, "The Divine Order to Marriage," Focus on the Family Ministries; https://www.focusonthefamily.com/marriage/gods-design-for-marriage/marriage-gods-idea/the-divine-order-to-marriage, accessed October 14, 2017.
2. Ibid.
3. Pierre Teilhard de Chardin, *The Phenomenon of Man* (Toronto, CA: Harper Perennial Modern Classics, 2008).
4. James A. Fowler, "No Independent Self: An Attempt at Clarification," Christ in You Ministries, 2005; http://www.christinyou.net/pages/noindependentself.html, accessed May 8, 2017.
5. *Parental inversion* occurs when a parent is unable or unwilling to fulfill the role and the child takes on the role of caretaker for the parent. The parentally inverted child will bear the weight of

care and responsibility that should rest on the parent. Unhealed parental inversion invariably leads to unhealthy relationships later in life. *Substitute mate* is a more serious form of parental inversion in which a parent relies inappropriately on a child of the opposite sex for emotional comfort or, in worst scenarios, for physical satisfaction.

Chapter 14

THE SCIENCE OF LOVE

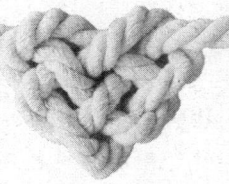

What we experience as emotions has a physiological basis. Scientists and medical doctors used to scoff at the idea that "unquantifiable emotions" could be given any consideration in serious medicine. However, the results of extensive research cannot be denied. To understand the *power* of emotions, it is helpful to understand the *biology* of emotion. Head and heart cannot be separated. *All* thoughts are connected to emotion. As a matter of fact, all *behavior* is connected to emotion.

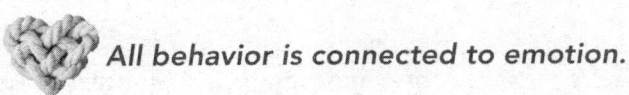

All behavior is connected to emotion.

MOLECULES OF EMOTION

There was little scientific understanding of emotions until researcher Candace Pert published her groundbreaking book *Molecules of Emotion* in 1999. Since that time, knowledge about the physiological basis for emotions and mood has exploded. Scientists now know that what we perceive as emotion is due to molecular signals read by our cells. *Neuropeptides*, or neurotransmitters, send emotional messages through our body on a cellular level. The word "neuropeptide" literally means nerve protein. When they encounter the surface of our cells, we experience a sensation we call *emotion*.

We experience physiological changes at the same time an emotion is triggered. We can feel cold with fear, blush with embarrassment, get a lump in the throat from shame, have a shaky voice when nervous, and experience muscular tension from anger. Our brain is in constant dialogue with our entire body through our emotions. Our head and heart are not just connected—they are unified in one system.[1]

 *Our head and heart are unified in one system.*

Have you ever heard someone describe a "hunch" or "gut" reaction—or felt a "knowing" in the gut? Police officers and firefighters learn to "go with their gut" and rely on more than just mental analysis. Our gut, bowels, or belly region is the place not only of emotion and will, but it is also inseparable from cognition or thought.

We have *feeling-thoughts*, or "emo-cognitions." Our memories are stored in long-term memory as indivisible units. When we retrieve thoughts and bring them into consciousness, the emotion emerges at the same time.

 *We have feeling-thoughts.*

LOVE OR FEAR

In the natural, emotions can be divided into two classes—love-based and fear-based. Love-based emotions promote good health, and fear-based emotions produce poor health. In the kingdom of God, we encounter a third class of emotions—*supernaturally good emotions*, or Spirit-born emotions!

When we experience emotions, signal molecules bombard the *cells of the body* with emotional information. The emotions are the communication system that speaks life or death to all the cells, organs, and systems of the physical body. For example, the emotion of *love* proclaims "life and security" to our cells while the emotion of *fear* says "death and danger." We must ask ourselves, "What am I telling the cells of my body through my emotions?"

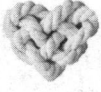 **The emotions are the communication system of the body.**

OPEN THE GATES

Our spirit and soul encounter God through the door of our heart. How do our cells encounter the love of God? Our cells have gates that open and close. The cell membrane is semi-permeable with protein *openings* allowing transport into and out of the cell. *Gates and channels* (receptors and effectors) allow the cell to receive, or absorb, what is in the surrounding environment.

Researchers have also discovered that certain receptors on our cells respond only to what they call *energy*—what we know as the spiritual energy of prayer.[2] Prayer changes our cells.

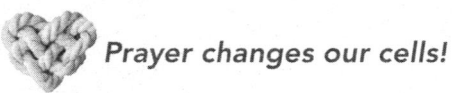 *Prayer changes our cells!*

When our cells encounter the power of God, the gates open and receive the glory of God. Our body understands the meaning of *"Lift up your heads, O you gates! And be lifted up, you everlasting doors! And the King of glory shall come in"* (Psalm 24:7). When you are in the presence of God, welcome Him to enter the gates of your cells.

A COMMUNITY OF CELLS

Whereas single-cell organisms "read" environmental cues directly and modify their behavior accordingly, our body is a community of cells that requires communication for cooperation. In community, specialized cells of the nervous and immune system bring the individual cells under the authority of a common plan of action. For example, the immune system is designed to fight off invaders that attack inside the organism as a whole rather than each cell having to defend itself in isolation.

 *Our body is a community of cells that requires communication for cooperation.*

In higher life forms, the brain has a specialized mechanism that enables our cells, systems, and organs to cooperate. The central nervous system and brain coordinate specialized "signal molecules" to maintain oversight of the whole organism. Cells yield their autonomy to the coordination of the brain.

Molecules of emotion keep the individual cells informed and synchronized, but the brain presides over the community. An organism's ability to maintain a constant internal balance is called *homeostasis*. Negative emotions, however, can disrupt the balance of our "community of cells" and set the stage for physical illness. Sickness and disease indicate that there are parts of our body not cooperating with the well-being of the whole.

THE SECOND BRAIN

Scientific studies demonstrate that we have an emotional "brain" in our gut that is as active and important as the brain between our ears. It is called the "second brain." Dr. Michael Gershon, researcher in the field of gastroenterology, published his revolutionary book on this subject in 1999, and it caused a tectonic shift in the biological sciences.[3] The second brain is our *enteric nervous system*.[4]

Experts in neurobiology and psychotherapy have defined a new field of research—*neurogastroenterology,* or "enteric neurology." Although we have a brain between our ears, God has given us a "second brain" with an equally significant function of emotional cognition, or *knowing,* in our gut. Have you ever heard anyone use the expression "I *know* that I know"? There are two places of knowing—head and heart.

 **There are two places of knowing—head and heart.**

Our two brains are connected by the left vagus nerve, which travels from our gut to the emotional center in the brain (the limbic system). Emotional information is also transmitted directly to the cells via neuropeptides, or "molecules of emotion."[5] The left vagus nerve primarily transmits emotional information *from the gut* to the brain, not the other way around. Our gut sends emotional information to our brain![6] The brain in our gut tells the brain in our head how we feel!

We instantly feel an emotion when we *think* about a painful experience. Our two "brains" experience the memory at the same time. We have *feeling-thoughts*, or "emo-cognitions," and *feeling-choices*, "emo-volition." Emotions rule both our thoughts and choices. It's a closed feedback loop that functions automatically...unless something from the outside breaks into the loop. When we pray, we allow God into the loop, and He changes us on the inside.[7]

 **The brain in our gut tells the brain in our head how we feel!**

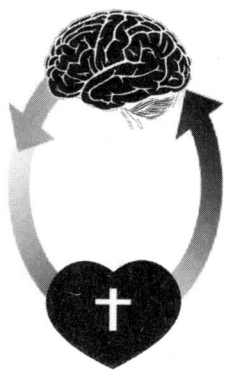

Emotion-Thought Loop. Our brain combines thoughts and emotions into indivisible units of *emo-cognition*. When an event is stored in the brain's long-term memory, it's saved as a feeling-thought entity, merged within the loop. Our mind and body operate as one system. Because the activity in the feedback loop is beyond our control, it continues to operate the same way despite our attempts to change.

When someone refers to something "pushing their buttons," their feeling-thought loop has been triggered, bringing a negative emotion to the surface. Every time that button is pushed, they react automatically and negatively. This can make it hard for people to change when it comes to their feeling-thoughts. It is not impossible, just hard.

Something from the outside must break into the loop to change the dynamics within the system. Otherwise, the same cycle keeps repeating itself. In the natural, brain mapping can change through use or disuse. Spiritually, that something is making a connection with God and receiving from Him.

 **Something from the outside must break into the loop to change it.**

Emotion-Will Loop. Not only is there an emo-cognition loop, but there is also an *emo-volition* loop. Emotions rule!

> [Scientists once] regarded emotion as elusive, objectively difficult to define, and thus, not acceptable to study.... As recent research has shown, this prejudice and attitude are profoundly wrong. In the very least, we can say that emotion is always in the loop of reason. Emotion is an adaptive response, part of the vital

process of normal reasoning and decision-making. It is one of the highest levels of bioregulation for the human organism and has an enormous influence on the maintenance of our homeostatic balance and thus of our well-being.

Emotion is a very adaptive form of physiological response, and it regulates our lives. Emotion is expressed largely in the theater of the body, through posture and facial expression as well as through such internal processes as heart rate and blood pressure....

We do ourselves a disservice when we think of human beings as exclusively logic- or knowledge-driven, and fail to pay attention to the role of the emotions. The two systems are enmeshed because that is the way our brain and our organism have been put together [during the process of embryonic development].[8]

 *Emotion regulates our lives.*

Our brain gives us the ability to connect with our heart for socialization. In other words, what we learn cognitively is linked with what we know emotionally so connections can develop and form *relationships*. Without this ability to link hearts with other people, we would live separate and isolated lives much like a hamster in a hamster ball,[9] moving around but never really making an emotional connection with other beings.

> [Brain] plasticity allows us to develop brains so unique in response to our individual life experiences that it is often hard to see the world as others do, want what they want, or to cooperate.... What nature provides, in a neuromodulator like oxytocin, is the ability for two brains in love to go through a period of heightened plasticity, allowing them to mold to each other and shape each other's intentions and perceptions. The brain...is fundamentally an organ of socialization, and so there must be a mechanism that, from time to time, undoes our tendency to become overly individualized, overly self-involved, and too self-centered.[10]

BRAIN CHANGERS

The brain has two types of pleasure centers—contentment and craving. Love triggers satisfying, contented pleasure. Lust triggers craving, exciting pleasure. Both change the brain and wire us for patterns of relationship. To understand the power of love and lust, it is helpful to understand the neuroscience behind these emotions. *Neuromodulators* are molecules of emotion that wash over the neurons in the brain and create changes in the brain mapping pertaining to relationships and social connections.

Oxytocin, the molecule of love, is a *neuromodulator*, or "brain changer." The brain can change even in adulthood. Love molecules stimulate the *contentment* pleasure center of the brain. Neuromodulators wash over the nerve cells in the brain, melting away some connections, strengthening others, and creating new ones. Love molecules create and strengthen relational ties. They actually change neurons and neural pathways in the structure of the brain itself.

Oxytocin reinforces bonding in mammals, attaches children to their parents, and is released when a husband and wife make love. It's also called the molecule of monogamy.

Characteristics of Oxytocin

- Creates a peaceful mood
- Increases trust
- Induces tender feelings
- Increases generosity
- Strengthens emotional attachments
- Brings down emotional walls
- Allows unlearning to take place

Love creates connections between human hearts and the brain. The only way to know love is to experience it. Receiving and giving love make us whole. Love makes it possible for us to live in society. Without emotional connectedness we are doomed to isolation.

 *Receiving and giving love make us whole.*

Mother and infant. Loving interaction between a mother and her baby teaches an infant the skills of life and love. Mother and infant learn one another's sounds, gestures, and facial expressions in a mutual emotional dance. A heart-to-heart attachment is created. In the process, the infant's limbic system (emotional center of the brain) and neural pathways form in the brain. The science of the brain points to the emotions of the heart. Love changes the structure of the brain. The love patterns learned in infancy and childhood are the models of relationship later in life.

 **The science of the brain points to the emotions of the heart.**

Father and family. Fathers not only experience a surge of oxytocin at the birth of their baby, but another molecule is released in males—vasopressin. It is known as the monogamy, or commitment, hormone. Vasopressin is "closely related to social bonds in males and also to defensive behaviors to preserve the self and family members."[11] In other words, it causes a man to want to protect his family and be there for them.

> The result of this increased hormonal activity is that bonding, attachment, protection, love, loyalty, commitment and caring are all enhanced in a new father. Thus science is showing us that a father with close, strong, intimate contact during pregnancy, birth and early infancy will be supported by [his emotions] during his early engagement in the family. Fathers are acquiring tenderness and a sense of belonging from engaging with mother and baby during pregnancy, birth and after. This then establishes a more durable foundation for a life-long loving relationship between father and child. Our society as a whole is also benefiting as a result of this transformation in fathers.[12]

CRITICAL LIFE STAGES

"Massive neuronal reorganization occurs...when we fall in love and when a baby is born."[13] A third instance of massive reorganization due to a flood of oxytocin occurs at the time of salvation. When we open the door of our heart to God, He gets in the feeling-thought loop! The salvation experience allows the supernatural love of God to be transmitted through our spirit and emotions for the first time, dramatically transforming our spirit, thoughts, choices, and emotions.

When our heart makes a connection with the heart of God, He causes our life to intersect with His Life. When we welcome Jesus into our heart, the natural molecules of love merge with the *supernatural* love of God. Thereafter, each time we connect with God in prayer, our spirit, soul, and body are changed by His love.

When we open the door of our heart to God, He gets in the loop!

THE LOVE OF GOD

When we welcome Jesus into our heart, we experience the *supernatural* love of God. The love of God floods our feeling-thought loop, transforming our thoughts, will, and emotions. Every time we connect with God in prayer, our spirit, soul, and body are impacted by His love.

Oxytocin has one other property that is highly significant for believers. It allows unlearning to take place so that our old view of ourselves can change when we begin to see ourselves through the eyes of someone who loves us.[14] This is true in human relationships, but how much more powerful it is when we begin to see ourselves through God's eyes. How does God see you? God sees you through eyes of love. You are the center of His attention and the apple of His eye!

> *Keep me as the apple of Your eye; hide me under the shadow of Your wings* (Psalm 17:8).

 **God sees us through eyes of love.**

INDIVIDUAL TRANSFORMATION

Love changes people. Oxytocin allows us to become different from the way we were in the past. Because of oxytocin, we can "unlearn" old perceptions and learn new ones. Whenever you spend time with God in prayer, you experience a measure of transformation!

> *But we all, with unveiled face, beholding as in a mirror the glory of the Lord, are being **transformed** into the same image from glory to glory, just as by the Spirit of the Lord* (2 Corinthians 3:18).

SPIRITUAL LOVE

Oxytocin gives us the means to open emotional doors and form close relationships in the realm of the spirit. Individuals are completely isolated from one another without relational bonds. Relational bonds are necessary or society could not exist. Christians have the astounding opportunity to form *supernatural relational bonds* with God and other believers by merging oxytocin with the fruit of the Spirit.

> *And above all these [put on] love and enfold yourselves with the **bond** of perfectness [which binds everything together completely in ideal harmony]* (Colossians 3:14 AMPC).

 **Believers form supernatural relational bonds with God and other believers by merging oxytocin with the fruit of the Spirit.**

Oxytocin and Unity

Only love makes unity possible. In Ephesians chapter four, Paul says that the purpose of ministers is to equip believers for spiritual *unity*.

> *I...beseech you to walk worthy of the calling with which you were called, with all lowliness and gentleness, with longsuffering, bearing with one another in love, endeavoring to keep the **unity** of the Spirit in the **bond** of peace* (Ephesians 4:1-3).

> *And He Himself gave some to be apostles, some prophets, some evangelists, and some pastors and teachers, for the equipping of the saints for the work of ministry, for the edifying of the body of Christ, till we all come to the unity of the faith and of the knowledge of the Son of God, to a perfect man, to the measure of the stature of the fullness of Christ* (Ephesians 4:11-13).

Prayer and the Physical Body

When we are born again, a spiritual transformation takes place. We become God-indwelt, a new creation! When we received forgiveness, we experienced peace with God for the first time. Although unbelievers can sometimes feel the peace of God in the atmosphere, Christians experience supernatural peace within. Because Jesus has given us His peace as a gift, it is always available for us (see John 14:27).

As soon as we are born again, we become a new creation spiritually, but the "new creation" *begins* to be imprinted on every cell. When our heart changes, our cells change: *"Therefore, if anyone is in Christ, he is a new creation..."* (2 Corinthians 5:17).

 **When our heart changes, our cells change.**

Scientific research has documented the positive impact of prayer on human physiology. Research indicates that prayer produces quantifiable positive effects on both our immune system and brain.[15] Every time we are in the presence of God, at least some healing occurs.[16] When we pray regularly, we create a healing environment for our entire being. We become less likely to become sick and also recover more quickly from surgery and illness.[17]

Prayer is more than talking to God. Prayer is being with God, spirit-to-Spirit. The Lord is not only our Savior and Forgiver; He is our Divine Healer and He dwells in our heart. Every time we are in the presence of God, we are changed.

The Lord—who is the Spirit—makes us more and more like him as we are changed into his glorious image (2 Corinthians 3:18 NLT).

PRACTICE
WELCOME GOD INTO YOUR PHYSICAL BODY

Welcome the presence of God into your physical body. Spend some time in prayer receiving His love into every part of you.

1. **Pray.** Prayer is fellowship with a Person. Come into the presence of the Divine Healer to honor Him.

    Pray. Close your eyes and pray, placing your hand on your belly.

    Focus. Focus on Christ within.

    Feel peace. Yield and feel peace.

2. **Receive**

    Pray. Close your eyes and pray, placing your hand on your belly.

    Yield. Yield to the Divine Healer in your heart.

    Receive. Welcome healing into your brain and every cell of your body.

3. **Soak**

    Time. Set aside a period of time—at least thirty minutes—and wait quietly in the presence of the Divine Healer within.

    Yield. Yield even more and go deeper in God. The more you open your spirit to God, the more healing occurs

Endnotes

1. John E. Sarno, *The Mindbody Prescription: Healing the Body, Healing the Pain* (New York: Warner Books, 1999), xviii-xxviii.
2. Bruce Lipton, *The Biology of Belief: Unleashing the Power of Consciousness, Matter and Miracles* (Santa Rosa, CA: Mountain of Love/Elite Books, 2005), 84, 99.
3. Michael Gershon, *The Second Brain* (New York: HarperCollins, 2003). Original work published 1999.
4. There are millions of neurons in the enteric nervous system as well as in the central nervous system (CNS) consisting of the brain, spinal cord, and peripheral nerves. Neurons line the walls of our esophagus, intestines, stomach, and colon. The left vagus nerve connects the brain's emotional center with the gut. Neuropeptides, molecules of emotion, are released throughout the body and brain, transmitting emotional information to every cell, organ, and system of the entire body.
5. Neuropeptides, molecules of emotion, are continuously released throughout our body and brain, transmitting emotional information to every cell, organ, and system. Our cells have receptors that "read" emotional information and react in a physiological response. For example, when we are embarrassed, we blush. Fear increases our heart rate. Sadness may cause us to cry.
6. Our physical heart doesn't *transmit* emotional information. It only *receives* emotional information and responds accordingly. It only has approximately 40,000 neurons that regulate our heart beat. You could think of the central nervous system and enteric nervous systems as powerful *computers,* but the physical heart is more like a *computer chip*.
7. A feedback loop is a closed system that functions automatically. Something from the outside must break into the loop to change the dynamics within the system. Otherwise, the same cycle keeps

repeating itself. Each person has a feeling-thought feedback loop that connects our head, heart, organs, and systems. Because the brain automatically links our thoughts and emotions together, it's impossible to separate them. They are inextricably joined as feeling-thought units.

8. Antonio R. Damasio, "The Science of Emotion," *Project on the Decade of the Brain* (May 5, 1998); http://www.loc.gov/loc/brain/emotion/Damasio.html, accessed October 2, 2010.
9. A hamster ball is a hollow clear plastic sphere into which small rodent pets such as hamsters or gerbils can be placed. It allows them to explore the environment outside their cages yet remain separate from it so they won't run away or get lost.
10. Norman Doidge, *The Brain that Changes Itself* (New York: Penguin Group USA, Inc., 2007), 120-121.
11. Sarina R. Saturn, "Flexibility of the Father's Brain," *Proceedings of the National Academy of Sciences of the United States of America*, 111(27) (July 8, 2017), 9671-9672.
12. Patrick Houser, "The Science of Father Love," Fathers to Be International (2009); http://www.fatherstobe.org/the science of father love.pdf, accessed October 17, 2017.
13. Doidge, The Brain that Changes Itself, 118.
14. Ibid., 121.
15. Randolph C. Byrd, "Positive Therapeutic Effects of Intercessory Prayer in a Coronary Care Unit Population," *Southern Medical Journal,* 81 (1988), 88-89; Harold G. Koenig, et al. "Modeling the Cross-sectional Relationships between Religion, Physical Health, Social Support, and Depressive Symptoms," *American Journal of Geriatric Psychiatry*, 5 (1997), 131-144; Harold G. Koenig and Andrew Futterman, "Religion and Health Outcomes: A Review and Synthesis of the Literature," Background paper, published in proceedings of *Conference on*

Methodological Approaches to the Study of Religion, Aging, and Health, sponsored by the National Institute on Aging (March 16-17, 1995).
16. Dale Mathews and Connie Clark, *The Faith Factor: Proof of the Healing Power of Prayer*, (New York: Penguin Group USA, Inc., 1998), 60-82.
17. Richard J. Davidson, et. al., "Alterations in Brain and Immune Function Produced by Mindfulness Meditation," Psychosomatic Medicine 65(4) (July-August 2003), 564-570.

Chapter 15

LUST AND BRAIN TRAPS

Love is about giving; lust is about getting. The molecule of emotion for lust and addiction, dopamine, stimulates the craving pleasure center of the brain. Dopamine pathways compete with oxytocin pathways for brain space; it simultaneously creates neural pathways of addiction in the brain and erases pathways of relationship. That is why a wife feels a growing distance if her husband has an affair or becomes involved with pornography. She is literally being erased from his brain.

 **Love is about giving; lust is about getting.**

Lust is...a strong desire for something or someone and is often used specifically regarding sexual desires. Lust is focused on pleasing oneself, often without regard for detrimental consequences. Lust is closely linked with greed. Many lusts or selfish desires are addressed specifically in the Ten Commandments, for example, where God's people were commanded not to desire a neighbor's house, wife, livestock, or possessions (Exodus 20:14-17).

In terms of lust related to sexual desire, Jesus directly addressed this controversial topic in His Sermon on the Mount. Jewish tradition often taught that only the action of adultery was sinful. Yet Jesus spoke more directly to the heart, teaching, *"You have heard that it was said, 'You shall not commit adultery.' But I say to you that everyone who looks at a woman with lustful intent has already committed adultery with her in his heart"* (Matthew 5:27-28). Lust is a sin in both thought and action. The cultural idea of, "It's okay to look if you don't touch" is not the teaching of Jesus.[1]

Pleasure principle. Exciting pleasure releases the neurotransmitter dopamine in the brain. The nucleus accumbens plays a central role in the reward circuit. Its operation is based chiefly on dopamine, which promotes desire, and serotonin, which increases the feeling of happiness. "The likelihood that the use of a drug or participation in a rewarding activity will lead to addiction is directly linked to the speed with which it promotes dopamine release, the intensity of that release, and the reliability of that release."[2] Dopamine may not just be the result of an addiction cycle. Dopamine may become the reward itself.

 *Dopamine may become the reward itself.*

The reward comes not from the activity or the substance being consumed, it comes from dopamine alone. The biochemistry of dopamine is the reward.... If you are addicted, then apparently you are not addicted to the substances and activities you crave, nor to the nicotine of cigarette smoke, the thrill of the roulette wheel, the gratification of sex, nor to the feelings of power. You are, in fact, addicted to the dopamine and its affects.[3]

DOPAMINE PATHWAY

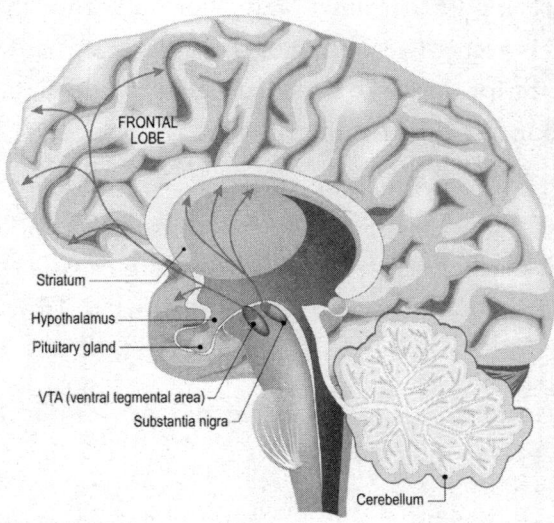

After the effects of dopamine wear off, another hormone called prolactin is released immediately. Prolactin causes the opposite effects of the dopamine high—feeling fatigued, irritable, and depressed. It leads to a cycle of highs and lows that destabilize the body and nervous system. Among numerous other undesirable effects, dopamine stimulates autoimmune diseases and speeds up cellular aging. The prolactin low fuels the need for another dopamine fix.[4]

Brain Traps. The reward circuit creates neural pathways in the brain that are more powerful than a habit loop alone. It is known as the addiction pathway. Our brain does not know the difference between a "bad" choice and a "good" choice in its decision-making process. It only knows that, if you are motivated, and if you make that same choice repetitively—like going to the bar after work every day—your neurons will literally connect in such a way as to support that inner-brain choice and thought pattern. Addiction is a repetitive pattern of choosing negative life options. It is difficult for people to break free because the brain neurons become connected and neural pathways are formed.

> *...I want to do what is right, but I can't. I want to do what is good, but I don't. I don't want to do what is wrong, but I do it anyway* (Romans 7:18-19 NLT).

 **Addiction is a repetitive pattern of choosing negative life options.**

The Stupids. When people get involved in sexual sin, it is common for them to lose the ability to make logical decisions, listen to reason, or even clearly understand Scripture or biblical principles. Although they may have been rational prior to engaging in sin, the presence of the demonic activity seems to give some believers "the stupids."

> *The path of the just is like the shining sun, that shines ever brighter unto the perfect day. The way of the wicked is like darkness; they do not know what makes them stumble* (Proverbs 4:18-19).
>
> *If any of you lacks wisdom, let him ask of God, who gives to all liberally and without reproach, and it will be given to him. ...But if you have bitter envy and **self-seeking** in your hearts, do not boast and lie against the truth. This wisdom does not descend from above, but is **earthly, sensual, demonic**. For where envy and **self-seeking** exist, confusion and every evil thing are there. But the wisdom that is from above is first pure, then peaceable, gentle, willing to yield, full of mercy and good fruits, without partiality and without hypocrisy* (James 1:5; 3:14-17).

Individuals also get the stupids when they have idols in their heart (Ezekiel 14:4), or agendas, and fantasize outcomes. Sometimes individuals invoke "God" to justify their religious-sounding (but not truly godly) reasoning, faith talk (denial), rituals, or bizarre remedies.

Hebb's Law. Neuroscientist Donald Hebb proposed a learning theory based on neuronal connections that form in the brain due to repetition. Hebb's law states: "neurons that fire together wire together." This creates a larger, more efficient pipeline for repetitive thoughts and actions. This plastic nature of the brain explains why people become used to making certain choices and why it becomes easier and easier to make those same choices again as time goes on.

Sometimes brain maps that should be separate merge. For example, when a guitarist moves two fingers together often enough, a condition called *focal dystonia* can result.[5] A single brain map "reads" the two fingers as one. If the musician attempts to move one finger, the other finger automatically moves.[6]

 **Neurons that fire together wire together.**

A therapist who works with such conditions proceeds in this manner: First, they must avoid the guitar for a while to weaken the brain map. Then hold a guitar with only one string, which they touch with a single finger. Next, a second string is used for the second finger to feel. This causes separate brain maps to reform for each finger. It is encouraging to recognize that the same neuroplasticity that creates a trap also provides a way out, even in the natural. How much more can change occur when God is brought into the equation!

Due to doctors and therapists who understand the brain's ability to change itself, patients have been able to recover brain functions damaged by injury, strokes, or disease in addition to changing undesirable patterns of behavior such as repetitively forming unhealthy relationships, addiction, and obsessive compulsive disorder (OCD).

> By the time A. went to college, he found himself replaying his critical-period experience [in early childhood] and being attracted to emotionally disturbed, already

attached women very much like his mother, feeling it was his job to love and rescue them. A. was caught in two plastic traps. The first was that a relationship with a thoughtful, stable woman who might have helped him unlearn his...[attraction to] problem women, and teach him a new way to love, simply didn't turn him on, though he wished it would. So he was stuck with a destructive attraction, formed in his critical period.

His second, related trap can also be understood plastically. One of his most tormenting symptoms was the almost perfect fusion in his mind of sex with aggression.... It was as though he lacked separate brain maps for sexual and violent feelings. ...I got him to search his experience to find...[instances] in which aggression or violence was untainted by sex. Whenever these areas came up a pure physical tenderness, or aggression that wasn't destructive I drew his attention to them. As time passed, he was able to form two different brain maps. ...By the end of therapy he was in a healthy, satisfying, happy marriage; his character, and his sexual type, had been radically transformed.[7]

If, even in secular therapy, there is a cure for brain traps, how much more can God deliver those who trust in Him! The Scriptures tell us to *"Flee sexual immorality"* (1 Corinthians 6:18) and that God will make a way of escape for us—we can rest assured of God's ever-present help.

Endnotes

1. "What Does the Bible Say about Lust? What Is Lust?" Compelling Truth; https://www.compellingtruth.org/what-is-lust.html, accessed March 15, 2017.
2. "Understanding Addiction: How Addiction Hijacks the Brain," Help Guide; https://www.helpguide.org/harvard/how-addiction-hijacks-the-brain.htm, accessed February 4, 2017.
3. David Bradley, "Could Dopamine be the Most Evil Chemical in the World?" *Chemistry Views* (October 3, 2011); http://www.chemistryviews.org/details/ezine/1340629/Could_Dopamine_be_the_Most_Evil_Chemical_in_the_World.html, accessed October 16, 2017.
4. Mary Jeanne Kreek, "Opioids, Dopamine, Stress, and the Addictions," *Dialogues in Clinical Neuroscience,* 9(4) (December 2007): 363-378; K. Ray and M. Wallis, "Effects of Dopamine on Prolactin Secretion and Cyclic AMP Accumulation in the Rat Anterior Pituitary Gland," *Biochemical Journal* 194(1) (January 15, 1981), 119-128.
5. Doidge, *The Brain that Changes Itself* (New York: Penguin Group USA, Inc., 2007), 106.
6. Ibid., 123-124.
7. Ibid.

Chapter 16

THE PORNOGRAPHY EPIDEMIC

According to statistics, the use of pornography has reached epidemic proportions. The word "epidemic" refers to the widespread occurrence of infectious disease in a population. Likening pornography to a societal disease indicates that it has become a quite serious problem. A number of states have introduced legislation declaring it a public health crisis.[1]

FANTASY RELATIONSHIPS

Lust is the emotion that drives the porn epidemic. Viewing pornography is a fantasy relationship for one-way sexual gratification. Based on scientific research, it is extremely harmful. It has a damaging effect on both the individual who gets involved with it as well as their relationships with others. In addition, pornography is highly addictive. The lust involved makes changes in the structure of the brain, just as in all addictive behaviors.

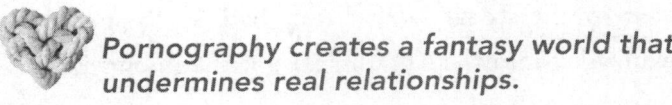

Pornography creates a fantasy world that undermines real relationships.

Dr. Norman Doidge, psychiatrist and neuroscientist at the Columbia Center for Psychoanalytic Training and Research in New York and the University of Toronto's department of psychiatry, states:

> [W]hen the Internet was growing rapidly and pornography was exploding on it, I treated or assessed a number of men who all had essentially the same story. Each had acquired a taste for a kind of pornography that, to a greater or lesser degree, troubled or even disgusted him, had a disturbing effect on the pattern of his sexual excitement, and ultimately affected his relationships and sexual potency. ...These were pleasant, generally thoughtful men, in reasonably successful relationships or marriages....They reported increasing difficulty in being turned on by their actual sexual partners, spouses, or girlfriends, though they still considered them objectively attractive. When I asked if this phenomenon had any relationship to viewing pornography, they answered that it initially helped them get more excited during sex but over time had the opposite effect. Now, instead of using their senses to enjoy being in bed, in the present, with their partners, lovemaking increasingly required them to fantasize that they were part of a porn script.
>
> Their sexual fantasy lives were increasingly dominated by the scenarios that they had, so to speak, downloaded into their brains. ...I got the impression

that any sexual creativity these men had was dying and that they were becoming addicted to Internet porn. ...The changes I observed are not confined to a few people in therapy. A social shift is occurring.[2]

PORN AND THE INTERNET

When the Internet revolutionized the home computer and the communications world in the mid-1990s, pornography became easily accessible in the privacy of one's own home. In addition, there was no downside such as an embarrassing interaction with a clerk in a store or the possibility of encountering or being seen by someone you know. Internet pornography promises all reward and no consequences. As a result, pornography *addiction* has become all too common.

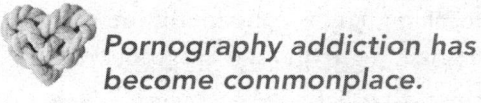
Pornography addiction has become commonplace.

A recent comprehensive analysis of 50 studies of pornography reveals that viewing porn diminishes men's sexual and relational pleasure significantly. "In an overall combined-sample analysis of relational and sexual satisfaction studies...the consumption of pornography was associated with lower interpersonal satisfaction."[3]

> The meta-analysis, [a statistical analysis that combines the results of multiple scientific studies], which included more than 50,000 participants from 10 countries, found clear and consistent results of diminished

interpersonal satisfaction directly tied to the use of pornography.

Dawn Hawkins, Executive Director of the National Center on Sexual Exploitation (NCOSE), praised the new research as making a significant contribution to the growing body of data showing the damage caused by pornography use.

"Pornography is sex-negative," Hawkins said in a statement made available to Breitbart News, because it "rewires an individual's sexuality to pixels on a screen rather than to a real person, which is inherently inconsistent with healthy, organic relationships...." "A wide body of research is bringing attention to the various ways pornography negatively impacts both women and men, and this latest meta-analysis contributes important findings to that on-going dialogue," she added.

According to NCOSE, Internet pornography consumption by adolescents is "associated with risky sexual behavior that can have profoundly adverse effects such as anal sex, multiple sexual partners, and substance use during sex." More importantly, however, is the harm porn causes to otherwise healthy relationships, as the new report underscores.[4]

STATISTICS

The general inundation of our culture by sex in media, sex education indoctrination in our schools, and the normalization of immorality is quite disturbing. Few individuals are able to reach adulthood unscathed by some sort of sexual activity, ranging from being a victim of molestation, indulging in childhood sexual curiosity, to getting caught up in pornography.

Pornography as a business

Family Safe Media reports that pornography is a $57 billion business worldwide and a $12 billion business in the U.S.[5]

- The Internet pornography industry generates $12 billion dollars in annual revenue– larger than the combined annual revenues of ABC, NBC, and CBS.[6]
- 87 percent of university students polled have virtual sex, mainly using Instant Messenger, webcam, and telephone.[7]

Women

Today's Christian Woman found in a survey that one out of every six women, including Christians, acknowledged struggling with the same addiction.

- A 2006 survey released by Internet Filter Review showed that 17 percent of women said they struggled with pornography addiction and that one in three visitors to pornography sites were women.[8]
- About 30 percent of Internet pornography consumers are women, according to the 2008 Internet Pornography Statistics.[9]

Children

Children between the ages of 12 and 17 make up the largest group of viewers of Internet porn.[10]

Of those arrested in the U.S. for the possession of child pornography between 2000 and 2001, 83 percent had images involving children between ages 6 and 12; 39 percent had images involving children between ages three and five; and 19 percent had images of infants and toddlers under age three.[11]

Approximately 20 percent of all Internet pornography involves children.[12]

Child pornography has become a $3 billion annual industry.[13]

There is an association between viewing child pornography and committing child sexual abuse.[14]

A study of The American Journal of Preventive Medicine found that one in six men reported being sexually abused as children. Almost 40 percent of the perpetrators were female.[15]

Christians

Research indicates that 47 percent of Christian families admit a pornography problem.[16] *Christianity Today*, winter 2005, reports that, according to pastors, the top sexual issues damaging to their congregation are:

- 57 percent pornography addiction
- 34 percent sexually active never-married adults
- 30 percent adultery of married adults
- 28 percent sexually active teenagers
- 16 percent sexual dissatisfaction

PORN'S EFFECT ON CHRISTIAN YOUTH

Josh McDowell, *The Porn Phenomenon*, states:

> About six years ago, I began to sense something was seriously wrong. I couldn't quite put my finger on it. Whatever it was, it was negatively affecting the receptivity of young people to the biblical faith that parents and churches so desperately want to pass on.
>
> After a lot of questions and investigation, I concluded that young people are being overwhelmed by Internet pornography. The easy access our kids have to pornography is distorting their views of morality and the Christian faith....
>
> When 54 percent of Christian young adults ages 18 to 24 seek out porn at least occasionally, and when two out of three youth pastors and more than half of senior pastors say porn is a current or past struggle, we have a genuine crisis on our hands. Porn is undermining God's truth in the lives of young people and eroding the credibility of the Church.
>
> Pornography is not new. However, the digital tools that deliver and propagate it today are new, and they have fundamentally changed the landscape. But not even the ubiquity and easy access of smartphone and tablet apps will be able to compete with the coming advancements in virtual reality (VR) technology. ...In the near future, [new technology with integrated

systems] will...bring...the user's body into the virtual space—meaning a user won't just see and hear but also touch and feel virtual objects and people as if they were real....

We need a culture among church leaders and parents that is more conducive to transparency and emotional safety, where Christians of all ages can admit their struggles. We need to extend more grace and offer greater hope: People *can* be restored by God's grace through the body of Christ.[17]

Addiction

Loss of control is the defining characteristic of addictive behaviors.

Addiction is the inability to stop consuming a substance or engaging in a behavior despite the adverse health and social consequences. Doctors now diagnose addiction under the umbrella of substance use disorders.

While anyone can develop a substance use disorder, some personal and medical factors can increase the risk of dependence.

The most obvious risk factor is taking an illicit or mood-altering substance, but a complex web of risk factors can contribute to addiction. Many substances that form the basis of addiction are not chemically addictive. This means that other elements can lead to substance use disorders.[18]

Pornography affects people physiologically, emotionally, and spiritually. The use of pornography is damaging to individuals, families, marriages, and, by extension, churches themselves.[19] It takes healthy individuals to have a healthy church!

> The use of pornography…weakens the church today in three significant ways: First, it creates a *dependency* on pornography that weakens the individual believer [spiritually]. Second, it causes a *disruption* of the "one-flesh" union that weakens Christian marriages. Third, it results in a *distortion* in thinking that weakens a Christian's ability to relate and function [in life in general, in the workplace, and in personal relationships].[20]

The good news is that those who are caught in the porn trap can escape! There is a way out. Even in the natural, therapists who have unlocked the secrets of brain plasticity are having good success freeing their patients from the trap of Internet porn.

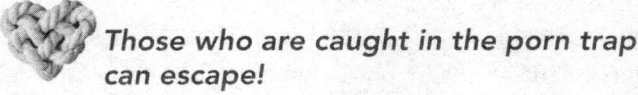

Those who are caught in the porn trap can escape!

> As for…patients who became involved in porn, most were able to go cold turkey once they understood the problem and how they were plastically reinforcing it. They found eventually that they were attracted once again to their mates. None of these men had addictive personalities or serious childhood traumas, and when they understood what was happening to them, they stopped using their computers for a period to weaken their problematic neuronal networks, and their appetite for porn withered away.…

[T]he same laws of neuroplasty that allow us to acquire problematic tastes also allow us...to acquire newer, healthier ones and...even to lose our older, troubling ones. It's a use-it-or-lose-it brain even where sexual desire and love are concerned.[21]

If neuroscience and the plasticity of the brain allow unsaved individuals to find freedom, how much easier should it be for believers with God's help. Using the first-feel-forgive prayer steps on the Blue Card (see chapter 7), pray through entry points and spend time in prayer welcoming the presence of God into any brain traps you might have.

Endnotes

1. Penny Nance, "Pornography Is a Public Health Crisis: Treat It Like One," *The Hill* (April 7, 2018); https://thehill.com/opinion/civil-rights/382067-pornography-is-a-public-health-crisis-treat-it-like-one, accessed October 24, 2018.
2. Doidge, *The Brain that Changes Itself,* 103-104.
3. Paul Wright, Robert Tokunaga, Ashley Kraus, and Elyssa Klann (2017), "Pornography Consumption and Satisfaction: A Meta-Analysis," *Human Communication Research*, (March 2017), 315-343.
4. Thomas D. Williams, "Report: Pornography Use Tied to Relationship Dissatisfaction," *Breitbart;* http://www.breitbart.com/big-government/2017/03/15/report-pornography-use-tied-to-relationship-dissatisfaction/, accessed March 15, 2017.
5. "Pornography Statistics," Family Safe Media (January 10, 2006); http://www.familysafemedia.com/pornography_statistics.html, accessed February 1, 2011.
6. Ibid.

7. "Campus Kiss and Tell," University and College Sex Survey (February 14, 2006); http://www.campuskiss.com/default.aspx?survey=show&homepage=true, accessed March 17, 2010.
8. Rachel Duke, "More Women Lured to Pornography Addiction," *The Washington Times* (July 11, 2010); http://www.washingtontimes.com/news/2010/jul/11/more-women-lured-to-pornography-addiction/, accessed March 2, 2013.
9. Ibid.
10. "Pornography Statistics," Family Safe Media (January 10, 2006); http://www.familysafemedia.com/pornography_statistics.html, accessed February 1, 2011.
11. "Child Pornography Possessors Arrested in Internet-Related Crimes: Findings from the National Juvenile Online Victimization Study," *Virginia: National Center for Missing and Exploited Children* (2005); http://us.missingkids.com/en_US/publications/NC144.pdf, accessed July 7, 2009.
12. Janis Wolak, Kimberley Mitchell, and David. Findelhor, "Internet Sex Crimes Against Minors: The Response of Law Enforcement," Virginia: National Center for Missing & Exploited Children (November 2003); http://www.unh.edu/ccrc/pdf/jvq/CV70.pdf, accessed September 3, 2010.
13. Jerry Ropelato, "Top Ten Reviews," *Top Ten Reviews, Inc.* (December 5, 2005); http://internet-filter-review.toptenreviews.com/internet-pornography-statistics.html, accessed July 7, 2010.
14. Candace Sullivan, "Internet Traders of Child Pornography: Profiling Research," New Zealand's Department of Internal Affairs (October 2005); http://www.dia.govt.nz/pubforms.nsf/URL/Profilingupdate2.pdf/$file/Profilingupdate2.pdf, accessed January 10, 2006.
15. Shanna R. Dube, Robert F. Anda, Charles I. Whitfield, David W. Brown, Vincent J. Felitti, Maxia Dong, and Wayne H. Giles,

"Long-Term Consequences of Childhood Sexual Abuse by Gender of Victim," *The American Journal of Preventive Medicine*, Vol. 28(5) (June 2005), 430-438.

16. "Pornography Statistics," Family Safe Media (January 10, 2006); http://www.familysafemedia.com/pornography_statistics.html, accessed February 2, 2011.
17. Josh McDowell, *The Porn Phenomenon* (Carol Stream, IL: Tyndale House Publishers, Inc., 2016), 5-6.
18. Timothy J. Legg, "What are the Risk Factors for Addiction?" *Medical News Today*, (October 26, 2018); https://www.medicalnewstoday.com/articles/323467.php.
19. Joe Dallas, "Darkening Our Minds: The Problem of Pornography among Christians," *Christian Research Journal*, Vol. 27, No. 03 (2004); Patrick Fagan, "The Quiet Family Killer: Pornography and Marriage," Townhall, (December 7, 2009); https://townhall.com/columnists/patrickffagan/2009/12/07/the-quiet-family-killer-pornography-and-marriage-n815443, accessed October 29, 2011.
20. Joe Dallas, "Darkening Our Minds."
21. Doidge, *The Brain that Changes Itself*, 131.

 *Section Five*

WALKING IT OUT

Chapter 17

CHURCH AS FAMILY

Because parents are often flawed, God made provision both for our healing *and* re-parenting. No matter what you have been through, God has help for you and is able to provide what you needed but didn't receive. Father God sent His own Son, Jesus, to die for us so we could receive His supernatural love and acceptance and restore faulty foundations. *"When my father and my mother forsake me, then the Lord will take care of me"* (Psalm 27:10).

 **God made provision for both our healing and re-parenting.**

God also has a plan for a *new* family, the household of faith. It is absolutely correct to talk about your church "home." That is exactly what it is designed to be. Ask the Lord to show you where He wants you to attend church.

> *God sets the solitary in families...* (Psalm 68:6).

> *He [Jesus] came and preached peace to you who were far away and peace to those who were near. For through*

> *him we both have access to the Father by one Spirit. Consequently, you are no longer foreigners and strangers, but fellow citizens with God's people and also members of his household* (Ephesians 2:17-19 NIV).
>
> *And let us consider one another in order to stir up love and good works, not forsaking the assembling of ourselves together, as is the manner of some, but exhorting one another...* (Hebrews 10:24-25).

The Scriptures teach many spiritual principles in types, allegories, and parables. Jesus often taught about the kingdom of God using parables about seeds, soil, wind, plant growth, and harvest. Jeremiah 17:7-8 compares believers to trees and describes the conditions required for healthy growth:

> *But blessed is the man who trusts me, God, the woman who sticks with God. They're like trees replanted in Eden, putting down roots near the rivers—never a worry through the hottest of summers, never dropping a leaf, serene and calm through droughts, bearing fresh fruit every season* (Jeremiah 17:7-8 MSG).

As we obey God, He proves Himself. It produces a trusting heart in us when we become confident in His goodness and faithfulness. When we are planted by the Lord, we are like trees planted by a river, whose roots go deep in the well-watered soil. Roots give us stability. Notice that healthy trees are not self-planted. They are planted by God! Many choose the church they attend based on personal preference. It's better to ask the Lord to show us where He wants us to attend church.

 **As we obey God, He proves Himself.**

The decision you make concerning where you are to be planted cannot be made on the basis of personal convenience. It must be based upon the principles that govern the kingdom of God.... I believe the Spirit of God desires to lead and guide us in the decision of the local church in which we are to be planted. God has a place that is just right for us and it will be exactly what we need in order to grow and mature in the Lord. He knows what type of ministry we need in order to be fruitful.[1]

Believers who thrive are planted in two ways. First, they are planted in Christ. They are "firm, solid, and well-rooted, being by faith engrafted into Christ, and bringing forth fruit suitable to the soil wherein they are planted."[2]

The next requirement for healthy growth is having a healthy church home. *"Strangers [Gentiles] shall stand and feed your flocks, and the sons of the alien [Gentile] shall be your plowmen and vinedressers"* (Isaiah 61:5 KJV). The word "flock" refers to church homes that provide life-giving spiritual nourishment and do the work of spiritual husbandry, *"plowmen and vinedressers,"* for healthy growth. Healthy trees are planted with other trees.

> *I will open rivers in desolate heights, and fountains in the midst of the valleys; I will make the wilderness a pool of water, and the dry land springs of water.* **I will plant in the wilderness the cedar and the acacia tree, the**

myrtle and the oil tree; I will set in the desert the cypress tree and the pine and the box tree together, *that they may see and know, and consider and understand* ***together,*** *that the hand of the Lord has done this...* (Isaiah 41:18-20).

The Lord plants many trees of various kinds together to make a sheltering forest. God brings us together with the people of His choosing to build His church so we can grow together. We were never intended to live isolated lives (see Hebrews 10:24-25).

A young woman attended our church for more than a year. A member of the congregation provided a place for her to live rent-free while she got on her feet financially. Numerous others helped her in many different ways. However, she never made a heart connection nor listened to sound advice. She kept moving from one job to another, never making enough to live on her own. Finally, she moved to another state unchanged and unappreciative of the help she had received. Those who fail to be planted are *"like a tumbleweed on the prairie... [they are] rootless and aimless in a land where nothing grows"* (Jeremiah 17:6 MSG).

God plants for *growth*. *"Grow in the grace and knowledge"* of the Lord (2 Peter 3:18). The Lord already knows where each one of us will grow best. A vital ingredient seems to be *heart commitment* to a family of believers. Therefore, we should earnestly ask the Lord to reveal which family of believers He has chosen for us. When we are planted in a healthy fellowship of believers, we become part of a family where we learn to love and serve one another.

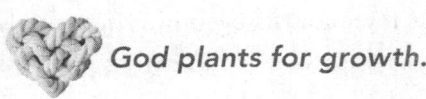 God plants for growth.

God plants for *provision*. Provision includes *all* our needs, not just finances. *"Seek first the kingdom of God and His righteousness, and all these things shall be added to you"* (Matthew 6:33). That includes proper relationships.

 God plants for provision.

God plants for *fruitfulness*. When we are planted and in fellowship with other believers the Scriptures encourage us to make our church family a priority (see Galatians 6:10). When we do, we grow spiritually and live blessed lives (see 1 Peter 1:22). Community has a way of working selfishness out of us and increasing love and compassion in us.

> *But the fruit of the Spirit is love, joy, peace, longsuffering, kindness, goodness, faithfulness, gentleness, self-control. Against such there is no law* (Galatians 5:22-23).

 God plants for fruitfulness.

As Jason has already shared in his testimony, the Lord rescued him after he backslid and made a major mess of his life. We promised Jason a place to stay in our home and assured him that God would provide. He had once been good with finances but fell into serious debt due to toxic relationships, hitting bottom quite dramatically. He arrived with not much more than the shirt on his back. Jason spent the first few months becoming spiritually healthy by turning his heart back to God and dealing with his internal issues, which also greatly improved his physical health.

Not only did Jason come into personal health, but he quickly became knit with our pastoral team and congregation and shared our passion to release spiritual how-to's to the body of Christ at large—our family mission. Before long, we ordained him and turned an area of our ministry over to him—TEAM Embassy. His teaching and preaching gifts have flourished, and he operates in a gift of discernment and discerning of spirits as a "watchman on the wall."

Jason has also established an online school that currently has more than 2,000 students enrolled from more than 54 nations around the world. The school has prospered and now provides a ministry income for him. The Lord then brought a lovely young woman to our church. She and Jason soon married and now have two precious children. Recently, the Lord visited Jason and brought him into personal revival that is releasing great spiritual refreshing to our entire congregation in a move of repentance and holiness.

Endnotes

1. Robert Gay, *Planted: Finding Your Place in the Church Today* (Lake Mary, FL: Creation House, 2004), 12-13.
2. John Wesley, "Isaiah 61," in *John Wesley's Explanatory Notes,* http://www.christianity.com/bible/commentary.php?com=wes&b=23&c=61, accessed September 14, 2017.

Chapter 18

REMAPPING THE BRAIN

As in any discipline, the old adage "use it or lose it" holds true. In the process of breaking a habit, pursuing physical or spiritual discipline, or gaining freedom from addiction, when our heart changes, our brain changes. As believers, we have the most powerful help of all—God! We have the supernatural power of God at work in our lives. Although the Lord moves in our lives in many different ways, we must do our own part while we yield to the supernatural.

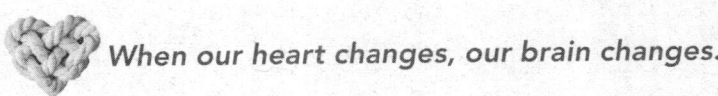

When our heart changes, our brain changes.

SUPERNATURAL DELIVERANCE

Deliverance from drugs. Drugs were an ever-present crutch in my (Dennis) unsaved days. It took scrounging around in a dumpster while people I knew drove by and waved to finally wake me up. That was pretty humiliating. Soon afterward, I got saved and the first thing I did was stuff all my weed down the garbage disposal while my head argued, "Are you crazy? At least sell it and make some money." The Lord delivered me in that very instant.

Deliverance from smoking. Never forget, we have a Divine Helper and access to divinely inspired change. Don't neglect any means God provides for your deliverance. You may be able to take some simple steps found in this book that will quickly cause change. Other habits may be more difficult to break. Dealing with some brain traps can take much prayer, deliverance, resisting, and time.

But don't discount the miraculous intervention of God! When I (Dennis) was less than six months old in the Lord, I felt God was telling me to stop smoking. (It was a three pack-a-day addiction and I always wore a shirt with a pocket for my cigarettes.) For three days I suffered withdrawal and continually slapped my chest feeling for a pack. The Lord prompted me to substitute a pocket Bible for the cigarettes. So, each time I slapped my chest, I pulled out the Bible, opened it, and read a verse. This went on for three days. On the fourth day I was completely delivered.

Don't discount the miraculous intervention of God!

Emboldened by my own victory, I turned to my family. (Don't try the following procedure unless you hear something like the audible voice of God speaking to you. I might have gotten punched!) Going over to my mom's house, I proceeded to pull a lit cigarette out of her mouth saying, "You don't need those anymore." She had been addicted to tobacco since she was 15 years old. My mom was instantly delivered.

Next, I prayed for another family member. Again, instant deliverance from cigarettes. A year or two later, she got angry at God and, in the throes of a temper tantrum, started smoking again. When she decided to quit again, it wasn't so easy. It took her two years and it was a long, laborious process.

Deliverance from alcohol. Then an elderly relative became my target. He drank excessively, to put it mildly. Mostly beer and wine. He washed down every meal with his own bottle of wine that he set beside him on the floor. I prayed for him and he instantly lost the taste for beer and wine and never drank again.

So much for the family. Now I ventured forth and went for a walk with an unsaved neighbor who was quite a heavy drinker. Right there on the sidewalk he got saved and was instantly delivered from alcoholism.

Later, after I began pastoring my first church, I went on a missions trip to Russian with a group of pastors. It was amazing how open the Russian people were and how many got saved. In a park in the middle of the day, we noticed a man who was quite drunk. As soon as I prayed for him, he was instantly sober and got saved.

Healed of Obsessive Compulsive Disorder (OCD). Dan, a man I had known for years was such a "neat freak" that it was an open joke. His father had been manic when it came to cleanliness and order. He enlisted his children in his quest for perfection, and ended up by convincing them that nothing was ever good enough. He passed on his compulsion to Dan who continued the pattern. He had a maid to clean while he was at work, but when he got home, he cleaned all over again. Whenever Dan went on vacation and stayed in a hotel, he purchased cleaning supplies and thoroughly cleaned the room before unpacking.

One day I had an opportunity to pray with Dan after he commented to me, "Have you ever driven halfway to work and then turned around because you were afraid you left the silverware drawer open?" Beginning to laugh, I exclaimed, "No! Never!" Wiping my eyes and continuing to chuckle, I then asked, "Could I pray with you about that? There must be a root." We prayed through a few issues about his dad. A few days later, Dan called with the sound of triumph in his voice. "I didn't have time to make the bed and went on to work anyway. I didn't feel the pressure in my gut and just thought, *Oh, well. That's okay!*"

LET GOD BE GOD

Don't discount any way the Lord wants to move in your life. Be open to everything He might provide as a means of deliverance for you. Moreover, as believers, our goal should be higher than just doing better or feeling better. The most wonderful thing about supernatural deliverance is that you then carry an anointing to set other people free.

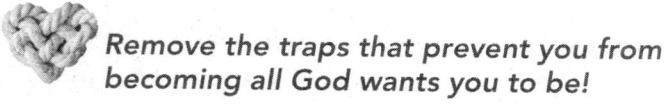

Remove the traps that prevent you from becoming all God wants you to be!

BRAIN REMAPPING

In *The Mind and the Brain: Neuroplasticity and the Power of Mental Force,* Dr. Jeffrey Schwartz writes that OCD sufferers recognize obsessive-compulsive thoughts and urges as separate from their intrinsic selves. For instance, after a few washings, the compulsive hand-washer realizes that his hands are clean and yet feels driven to keep washing them. It was reflection on this difference between the obvious truth (the hands are clean) and the irrational doubts (they might still be dirty) that prompted Schwartz to reassess the philosophical underpinnings of neuroscience.[1]

Schwartz discovered from brain scans that some regions in the brain of OCD patients showed unusual patterns of activity. He then had the patients engage in some concentrated mental effort that he called Relabeling, Reattributing, Refocusing, and Revaluing, or the 4 R's.

Schwartz documents not only that patients who undertook this therapy experienced considerable relief from OCD symptoms, but also that their brain scans indicated a lasting realignment of brain-activity patterns. Thus, without any intervention directly affecting their brains, OCD patients were able to reorganize their brains by intentionally modifying their thoughts and behaviors. The important point for Schwartz here is not simply that modified thoughts and behaviors permanently altered patterns of brain activity, but that such modifications resulted from, as he calls it, "mindful attention"—[or taking]...the stance of a detached observer.[2]

DAILY FOUR "R" STEPS[3]

1. ***Relabel.*** Recognize that the intrusive thoughts and urges to behave a certain way are caused by the brain trap.
2. ***Reattribute.*** The power of the thought or urge comes from the brain trap.

3. ***Refocus.*** Focus on something else for a few minutes at least. Do some other behavior in the meantime.
4. ***Revalue.*** Realize that the urge and thought don't have authority over you. They're not your boss and you're not their slave.

The first three steps allow you to see the OCD as separate from "you." When you put an emotional distance between yourself and the OCD, you refuse to own it. That allows you to deal with it more effectively. It separates "you" from "it." When you Revalue, you refuse to respond to the urge because it's not worth a response on your part. In other words, you would flee from a five-alarm fire but not a lit match. According to Schwartz:

> The goal of the first three steps is to use your knowledge of...the brain to help you clarify that this feeling is not what it appears to be and to refuse to take the thoughts and urges at face value, to avoid performing compulsive rituals, and to Refocus on constructive behaviors. You can think of the Relabel and Reattribute steps as a team effort, working together with the Refocusing step. The combined effect of these three steps is much greater than the sum of their individual parts.
>
> The process of Relabeling and Reattributing intensifies the learning that takes place during the hard work of Refocusing. As a result, you begin to Revalue those thoughts and urges that...would invariably lead you to perform compulsive behaviors. After adequate training

in the first three steps, you are able in time to place a much lower value on the OCD thoughts and urges.[4]

PRACTICAL MEASURES

Become accountable. Find a trustworthy partner with whom you can confide. Check in with that person on a regular basis in an open and honest way. (It may help to create a written schedule.)

Identify and avoid triggers. Addictive compulsions are often associated with triggers, or certain stimuli that increase desire to engage in the unwanted behavior. Triggers are associated with prior memories or situations that resulted in turning to the addictive behavior. These can include people, places, and emotional pressure. When breaking out of undesirable cycles, it is a good idea to minimize exposure to these triggers. Note that some triggers may be simple while others are more complicated. Common triggers include:[5]

- Stress
- Anger
- Frustration
- Depression
- Certain people
- Smells
- Songs
- Places
- Dates (such as holidays or anniversaries)

Make a list of environmental, emotional, and social triggers that operate in your life so you can choose alternatives in times of temptation.

1.

2.

3.

4.

5.

6.

When you have identified your triggers, make a plan to deal with them. This may include calling someone, taking the four "R" steps to shift your focus, writing down the trigger and deciding how you choose to respond, or physically moving to another location.[6]

Strengthen relationships. Work on your relationships with your spouse (if you are married), friends, and church family. Spend quality time with them.

Beware of the snare effect. It is vital to remember that a habit loop doesn't disappear. The snare that trapped us is still lying in wait. Therefore, we must be vigilant. Not worried, but vigilant. That way we don't become smug about our good behavior. We also don't give in to self-pity and shame when we blow it. Pride trips us up but humility keeps us in the grace of God: *"God resists the proud, but gives grace to the humble"* (James 4:6).

A stumble is not a disaster. Maintain an emotional distance that separates you as a person from the brain trap. That way when you slip up, you can say, "Oops, 'it' got me again but it's not keeping me there." 1) Admit you messed up but don't wallow in it. 2) Face your "pain" but forgive yourself. Don't give in to condemnation, guilt, or shame. 3) Get back up and keep walking. 4) Learn from it. For example, "I can't leave a plate of cookies out on the kitchen counter all afternoon without being tempted to snack." 5) Do right. Go right back to your plan again.

In Micah 7:7-9 in the Message translation, we find a scriptural stance to take in times of failure.

> *But me, I'm not giving up. I'm sticking around to see what God will do. I'm waiting for God to make things right. I'm counting on God to listen to me. Don't, enemy, crow over me. I'm down, but I'm not out. I'm sitting in the dark right now, but God is my light. I can take [it].... But it's not forever. He's on my side and is going to get me out of this. He'll turn on the lights and show me His ways. I'll see the whole picture and how right He is.*

Let's break this passage down to our personal level:

- I will look to the Lord and get my eyes off myself. *"But me, I'm not giving up. I'm sticking around to see what God will do"* (v. 7).

- The God of my salvation is here to help me. *"I'm waiting for God to make things right. I'm counting on God"* (v. 7).

- The habit is my enemy, but when I fall, I'll get back up. *"I'm down but I'm not out* (v. 8).

- I'm going to learn from this. *"He'll turn on the light"* (v. 9).

- I'll face my disappointment but give it to God. *"And show me His ways"* (v. 9).
- I won't lose hope. *"I'll see the whole picture"* (v. 9).
- I'll do what I know to do! *"Our soul has escaped as a bird from the snare of the fowlers; the snare is broken, and we have escaped"* (Psalm 124:7).

Endnotes

1. William A. Demski, "The Mind and the Brain: Neuroplasticity and the Power of Mental Force," First Things (May 2003); https://www.firstthings.com/article/2003/05/the-mind-and-the-brain-neuroplasticity-and-the-power-of-mental-force, accessed March 15, 2010.
2. Eda Gorbis, "Dr. Jeffrey Schwartz's Four Steps," Westwood Institute for Anxiety Disorders; http://hope4ocd.com/foursteps.php, accessed March 25, 2017.
3. Ibid.
4. Ibid.
5. "Identifying and Managing Addiction Triggers," Summit Behavioral Health; https://www.summitbehavioralhealth.com/resources/articles/identifying-and-managing-triggers, accessed January 30, 2017.
6. Eda Gorbis, "Dr. Jeffrey Schwartz's Four Steps."

Chapter 19

Restoration

Jason's Story

Our sin not only messes up our lives but it separates us from the presence of God: *"Your iniquities have separated you from your God; and your sins have hidden His face from you..."* (Isaiah 59:2). Besides being connected with my church family, a unique "tool" used by my dad's ministry made more difference in my restoration than anything else: *The 60 Day Challenge*.[1] Actually, *tool* may be the wrong word because what it really does is teach you to go to Christ within and let Him heal and restore your heart. It's not counseling but learning to rely on your own relationship with God.

> *We use our powerful God-tools for smashing warped philosophies, tearing down barriers erected against the truth of God, fitting every loose thought and emotion and impulse into the structure of life shaped by Christ* (2 Corinthians 10:4-5 MSG).

It's without a doubt the best thing for restoring believers that I have ever seen, or should I say experienced, because in encountering *The 60 Day Challenge,* God encountered me and turned me completely around to know Him face-to-Face.

Breaking Soul Ties

> *And you will seek Me and find Me, when you search for Me with all your heart. I will be found by you...* (Jeremiah 29:13-14).

When individuals have become involved with serious sin, they need a period of restoration. Forgiveness is instant. Restoration is a process! How to successfully restore is the problem. The church does not have a good history in the area of restoration. Church members are typically shamed and go to another church, move out of the area, or drop out of church entirely. Sometimes, they find a church that teaches license so they can continue in their sin without confrontation, healing, or a true work of the cross. Traditionally, leaders who fail or become burned out are removed from ministry, required to undergo counseling, and sit and do nothing for a period of time, usually several years. This has not worked well. Time does not heal wounds. Humiliation and forced inactivity do not restore. Unfortunately, too few ministers fully recover and return to active ministry. Many never learn how to deal with the root issues that caused them to fail.

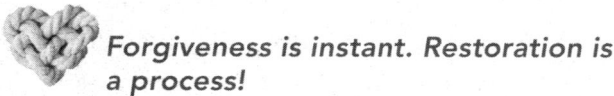

Forgiveness is instant. Restoration is a process!

The way to restore and the length of restoration depend upon type of sin and length of involvement. If a person has fallen into sin but does not have a prolonged history of indulgence, restoration can occur more quickly.

SINFUL BEHAVIOR

When dealing with sin, two major factors must be considered. Is it an isolated incident or is there a repetitive cycle?

1. Isolated Sin

Many individuals have childhood wounds that have given the enemy legal ground to tempt and harass them. In such cases, they may have been able to resist by willpower for a prolonged period of time before falling. The person should forgive, receive forgiveness and cleansing, and break soul ties when necessary. Then pray through childhood roots that made them susceptible. Restoration could take place in a relatively short period of time, perhaps a few months.

2. Repetitive Sin

The number-one factor is this: Do they want to change? Repetitive sin indicates that addiction may be involved, in which case neural pathways have formed in the brain. A person who is engaged in habitual sin needs multiple prayer sessions to deal with root issues. However, for a person to be healed, delivered, and restored, the habit loops and addictive pathways must also be re-modulated by the formation of new, spiritually healthy relational pathways. This takes place within the context of a loving and supportive church body.

- Does the person genuinely want to change?
- Repetitive sin indicates that addiction may be involved, in which case neural pathways in the brain have formed. A person who is engaged in

- habitual sin needs multiple prayer sessions to deal with root issues.
- However, for a person to be healed, delivered, and restored, the addictive pathways must also be re-modulated by the formation of new, spiritually healthy relational pathways.
- This takes place within the context of a loving and supportive church body.

THE 60 DAY CHALLENGE

For many years we have been teaching believers how to be healed of toxic emotional baggage by yielding to Christ within their own hearts. Thousands of lives have been transformed. Every believer can learn how to deal with unhealthy emotions and experience inner transformation.

The 60 Day Challenge started with me (Jennifer). It changed my whole life and since that time it has brought healing to countless others. The following is my story.

The weekend that we met for the first time, I (Jennifer) saw Dennis pray with an extremely distraught woman at a Christian conference. The woman, Amanda, had an emotional meltdown and collapsed on the floor weeping.

Everyone froze in their tracks. I was watching this take place and then thought to myself, *Five or ten years of counseling might help such a broken soul.* But this was before I met Dennis and learned these simple steps of forgiveness.

Dennis knelt beside Amanda, who had become hysterical. He began to coach her step-by-step, walking her through this simple process of supernatural forgiveness. Christ the Forgiver quickly and easily dealt with her emotional pain. In less than ten minutes, Amanda was up on her feet, smiling and calm, testifying that her emotional pain was gone.

Astounded, I understood that the rapid healing steps I witnessed could bring emotional healing to a world full of hurting people—including the most "mature" Christians still carrying wounds from childhood or battling daily stress at work, in ministry, around the family dinner table, or at school. I realized that whatever Dennis had done was a much faster and more thorough approach than anything I had ever witnessed before.

Dennis and I quickly became friends, then friendship turned to romance and we were soon married. For the first two months of our marriage, I asked Dennis to begin mentoring me in all the Lord had taught him, so he prayed with me regularly for a couple of months. He asked me to close my eyes and pray, then let the Lord bring anything to mind that needed to be dealt with. In a short period of time, God completely cleaned up the baggage of my past. It was so life-changing that I could barely recall how wounded I'd been before. I can hardly even remember the pains and fears that were once my constant companions. The fruit of this extraordinary transformation has manifested in a lifestyle of peace and closer walk with God.

Dennis had never before explained to anyone what he did internally to process issues. But because he loved me and I really wanted to understand, he described the steps. For example, the first evening we prayed he told me to close my eyes, put my hand on my belly, and pray. Then he explained that the epicenter of spiritual activity was in the gut.

As I cooperated with him, I opened my heart to Christ within. Dennis explained, "The peace you're feeling, that's the peace of God. Whenever we're in God's presence, we feel His peace. Now yield to Him more. That "bubble" you feel in your gut, that's joy—the fruit of the Spirit of joy." I was amazed to discover that we can tap into the fruit of the Spirit so easily. Prior to this, the fruit of the Spirit was just a mental concept to me like fruit on a bulletin board in Sunday school.

All the books and materials we have produced came out of Dennis' explaining spiritual truths to me in such a way that I could enter into the experience for myself. I just documented how the Holy Spirit works and how we cooperate with Him.

It's that simple. We cooperate with God and meet with Him in our heart. It's not just for a special few. Every believer has the same spiritual equipment and can learn to go directly to Christ within. Even little children can learn this. That's why I know that my story can become your story, too.

Later, we created a prayer journal and some prayer coaching CDs so others can go through the same process I went through, with some helpful tools that are now available on our website, www.forgive123.com. *The 60 Day Challenge* is also available as a course on the online school Jason designed at https://training.teamembassy.com/.

When people ask, "Where do I start," we always point them to *The 60 Day Challenge* whether they are new members of our church or a person in need of restoration. Because not everyone can have someone sit down regularly and pray them through issues, we wanted a way to help people go through the process on their own and that's why we created *The 60 Day Challenge*.

Keys for Restoration

Genuine, relational bonding. Restoration should include the formation of close, loving relational bonds. Ideally, this requires the individual to become *planted* in a church, not just "doing some time waiting" until the restoration period is over. It has to be genuine bonding. (Some individuals receive help when they form close and accountable relationships in a support group.)

Time spent in prayer. The *need* for restoration is clear evidence of spiritual distance from God. This can only be remedied by spending much time in abiding prayer. In this way, God can restore the spiritual heart and the physical brain.

Confidentiality. People who aren't part of the problem or part of the solution don't need to know. In most cases, restoration can be done discreetly.

Prayer for roots. Prayer should include the elements of deepening their personal relationship with God as well as healing for the heart. An individual in need of restoration should have regular times of prayer to deal with their root issues. They can do most of this on their own but it's a good idea for them to check in with someone to share how they're doing.

Accountability. Establish a system for accountability with a partner or trusted group.

Give them something to do. Just sitting but doing nothing doesn't restore an individual. After a few months of genuine repentance and progress in dealing with root issues, allow them to do something that is fulfilling to them. For example, a fallen pastor could be allowed to teach a class under supervision, or a musician could be given the freedom to sing in a group.

A Final Word of Encouragement

Remember, God never overwhelms us but leads us step-by-step into freedom and victory. Every baby step of obedience builds spiritual authority. Once we are free, we have an anointing to rescue others who are ensnared. *"He makes me as surefooted as a deer, enabling me to stand on mountain heights"* (Psalm 18:33 NLT).

Endnote

1. *The 60 Day Challenge* journal is available in two versions along with companion coaching CDs. It is also available on the online school website http://training.teamembassy.com.

About the Authors

Drs. Dennis and Jennifer Clark minister together as a husband and wife team and are Senior Pastors of Kingdom Life Church in Fort Mill, South Carolina. They are also founders and directors of Full Stature Ministries and TEAM Embassy School. Dennis holds a PhD in Theology and Jennifer holds a ThD in Theology as well as BS, MS, and EdS degrees in psychology. Jason Clark, Dennis' son, graduated from Blue Ridge Bible College in Rocky Mount, Virginia, and currently serves as Senior Associate Pastor at Kingdom Life Church and Chancellor of TEAM Embassy. Visit the authors online at www.forgive123.com.

Experience a personal revival!

Spirit-empowered content from today's top Christian authors delivered directly to your inbox.

Join today!
lovetoreadclub.com

Inspiring Articles
Powerful Video Teaching
Resources for Revival

Get all of this and so much more, e-mailed to you twice weekly!

LOVE TO READ CLUB
by **D DESTINY IMAGE**